Other books by Christina Chitenderu Mthombeni

Raising Better Children: Key to effective Parenting

# Imperfect Happy Marriage

## A Positive Outlook on Marriage in the 21st Century

Christina Chitenderu Mthombeni

Order this book online at www.trafford.com
or email orders@trafford.com

Most Trafford titles are also available at major online book retailers.

Scripture quotations marked NIV are taken from the *Holy Bible, New
International Version*®. NIV®. Copyright © 1973, 1978, 1984 by International
Bible Society. Used by permission of <u>Zondervan</u>. All rights reserved. [<u>Biblica</u>]

Print information available on the last page.

ISBN: 978-1-4907-5903-6 (sc)
ISBN: 978-1-4907-5905-0 (hc)
ISBN: 978-1-4907-5904-3 (e)

Library of Congress Control Number: 2015906274

*Trafford rev. 04/24/2015*

www.trafford.com

North America & international
toll-free: 1 888 232 4444 (USA & Canada)
fax: 812 355 4082

# Contents

# Acknowledgements

I would like to express my sincere gratitude to the four dear and lovely couples who allowed me into their marital space to talk about their journeys in marriage.

The family Life Department at Luton Central Adventist Church and the Adventist South England Conference for the inspiration through involving me in family focused seminars and workshops.

Dr R. Mano and her husband Mr. C. Mano for the very long marriage conversations we always share. For the advice and the continued support.

My sweetheart Courage, for all the different contributions towards the successful publication of this book, the patience and continued support.

Tanya, the apple of my eye, for allowing mummy to isolate herself while working on this book.

# Dedication

I dedicate this piece of work to my darling husband Courage, who gave me the opportunity to become a wife.

To Tanya Kagiso, our lovely daughter, carry this as a legacy when you are grown from mummy's heart.

My family, beloved siblings and their families.

My dearest friends of all times Winnet and Etelvina and their families.

Our long time family friends the Tilbury's.

# Introduction

Every human being desires and deserves to be happy in life. Happiness is the reason that drives people to wake up early and work hard for their life. It is finding fulfilment and satisfaction in one's own life. This book has its overall objective as to navigate the importance of finding happiness in marriage even through difficult times. The book also focuses on the complexity of marriage in the 21st century and how best married couples can deal with the modern marital challenges.

There are many different reasons why people get married. I read an article in Psychology Today which highlighted the fact that it is not always out of pure love that people get married. It is true in so many ways. People sometimes get married because of age and what they call 'the biological clock is ticking', the need to have children within a certain period of time, some people marry just to follow suit with their peers who are married. Others get married for financial stability and security, and sadly some get married out of arranged/forced marriages by family, church or community. I have said 'sadly' because in most cases there is no choice from either one party or both parties. However quite a lot of people also get married out of pure love.

With all the reasons of marriage highlighted above, comes the reality. When we look at marriage from either of the driving factors, we realise that there is no type of marriage guaranteed of perfection. In 1 Corinthians 7:28. Yet those who marry will have worldly troubles. The bible clearly states that any marriage is bound to face trying times. The success of it depends on how each married couple choose to deal with their marital troubles.

The percentage rise in the divorce rate worldwide is quite alarming. For every marriage, there is a fifty percent chance of divorce or separation before reaching two years of marriage. As painful as it sounds, marriages today are facing and experiencing what I can call, **'The tempest of marriage'**. Marriages are being attacked left right and centre by many different forces which in some cases seem small yet quite destructive to the marital union.

The new world has taken over and the challenges we face have made many create a different perception and outlook on marriage. If we look at the way our forefathers used to handle marriages, we might not be able to even pin point the actual problems they had. Back then, marriage was treated as a very important and sacred institution. When I was getting married, my grandmother said to me, 'Never treat marriage like a jacket which you put on during winter time and throw away when it gets hot'. My grandmother's point was for me to be prepared to face challenges in my marriage without resorting to giving up even when faced with extreme challenges.

# Chapter 1

# UNCONDITIONAL LOVE

Love is the stronghold of any relationship. It is the power behind the laughter, the touch, the forgiveness, the sense of belonging and the fulfilment and all other good things that we find in a relationship. As I highlighted in the introduction, it is not always the love that drives people into marriage, however love is the most important component in any relationship. The absence of love can present challenges which may threaten the marriage union.

There are a lot of cases where love is abundant but nothing else complements the marriage, this may also threaten the marriage.

Loving your spouse is not a duty and I believe it should not feel like it, but a mutual feeling and understanding of one's heart and feelings.

There are gestures of love that married couples show as a way of assurance and love for each other. People are created and moulded differently and the ways that couples show love to each other may differ. I have come across a lot of couples who feel that even if they show love gestures like, use of beautiful words or prepare a great romantic night out, they do not get any appreciation or recognition from their spouse.

The lack of recognition and appreciation can vehemently water down the drive to show love. When a marriage survives without showing each other the love, it can potentially distance the connection between couples. Loving and showing love to your spouse creates the need to be close and to be with each other. Marriage revolves around what you do with and for each other.

Loving each other can also be shattered by certain weaknesses, characters and personalities that each spouse possesses. For example realising that your spouse has been cheating on you or is flirting around can automatically reduce the level and the power or energy to show love to your spouse. She is not a super woman, neither is he a superman, every marriage faces different kinds of challenges and it comes down to how you choose to handle them as a couple.

Creating an environment of love in the home is a blessing and does not only carry the impact to you but to the children, families and friends. It motivates focus in the marriage and it gives all the reason after a hard day's work to go home and be with your wife or husband.

Couples create their love environment differently. The most important step is for each couple to understand the need for creating a loving environment in the marriage. The understanding of it as a need puts both of you to work.

When I grew up, my parents always had two constant quality times together even in their old age. They would wake up early each morning and have a chat in their room, we would always hear them laugh. They also used to eat together to the extent that even before my dad arrives home in the evening, we would all have our dinner but my late mum would wait for dad. Equally when my mum was not around, my father struggled to eat especially when mum went away for a few days.

By that time, I personally did not understand why someone could not eat in the absence of the other, but I later realised that they created an environment where their life kind of depended on each other and revolved around each other.

Showing love does not require money to buy expensive gifts or to go away to places where you need to pay.

Creating an environment of love is in the mind, therefore you deal with what you have and can afford.

I can still express that, a loveless marriage is like a lifeless body, it cannot function. Learning to love your spouse even under immense disappointments, hurt and anger can help you to heal within. Many spouses conform to a miserable marriage, where they are not treated with love and consideration. They conform to it because it is the only life and the only way they know.

## Real Life Story (pseudo names used)

Marissa and Keith fell in love in high school, they went to college together, finished and started to plan their future. The love they shared was so enormous and to them it felt endless like the horizon, Keith's sun shone on Marissa's forehead and Marissa's sun shone on Keith's forehead, they were inseparable and loved each other's heartbeat.

The few hurdles that the two faced were solved amicably because they did not want to waste time dwelling on the negative. They constantly reminded each other of how blessed and privileged they were to have found each other.

They finally made a decision to take on the commitment of marriage because they felt that they were ready and fit for each other. The wedding preparations began and their families were delighted to see their children taking a bold step in their lives, a proud moment for the parents and family.

As the preparations were underway, like any other normal wedding preparation, stress and anxiety kind of kicks in because most couples realise at this stage that they differ in many ways. Be it simple preferences, colours, setting e.t.c. Keith and Marissa were not an exception to this challenge. Marissa particularly wanted a talk of the town wedding, a wedding of flamboyance and wanted her wedding to fit that of a princess. On the other hand Keith was more of a conservative, live within your means and simplicity is classy kind of person. He focused more on the after wedding party life than the wedding event itself.

They drew up a budget for the needs of the wedding and one thing that hit them was that the budget was way higher than what they had set aside for the wedding. They decided to cut on some of the things that they thought would not affect the wedding process if not acquired. Three quarters of the cut backs were from Keith's side because Marissa could not do away with what she desired to have on her wedding.

To keep the peace, Keith had to succumb to the needs of his sweetheart but still the budget was strained, so they opted to take a loan towards the wedding day.

During the course of preparations, they also had to deal with each of the family's expectations. Each family had a guest list of their own and a list of wants as well. This further created more pressure on the young couple to the extent that by the time they had their wedding, their minds were not fully focused on the one most important thing –LOVE for each other.

The wedding day came and passed. Families and friends were ecstatic and overwhelmed with joy and pride on the newlyweds.

It took no time for Keith and Marissa to realise that they were actually in debt after the wedding. Their initial focus was then to strategise and find a way to clear the debt so that they could lead a debt free life and plan to have children. The debt that they had incurred would take them a little more than a year to clear.

This burden infuriated both as it was hindering them from actually fully enjoying each other and their married life. As many couples would experience in moments of distress, the blame game started. Keith started to make comments that implied, if Marissa had not pushed for an expensive gown, shoes and cake, they would be in harmony financially.

On the other hand Marissa expected Keith to understand and just deal with it. It got to a point that each time they had a conversation about anything else, one way or the other the topic would end up being about finance and the wedding bills.

The heart is a fragile component of love, the more bitter and unresolved arguments you have, the more the heart makes a dent and creates a distance slowly but surely.

The pressure for this couple mounted and mounted overtime, the arguments and blame escalated to the point that no one even cared how much hurt was inflicted on the other. Keith and Marissa's once happy life had simply vanished and their future was bleak. Marissa found solace in her work mates who included male colleagues. In the process of trying to find a shoulder to cry on, she secretly fell in love with one of her colleagues. So, each time they had an argument, she would speak to him and send him texts as a way of comforting herself.

One morning they woke up and decided that they did not expect their married life to be such hell, unloving and selfish, full of arguments. They never dreamt that one day they would wake up each morning and not look forward to spending time with each other. It never dawned on them that one day infidelity was going to visit their relationship.

Life became so unbearable for Keith when he also realised Marissa had found comfort in another man's arms. He could not take it, neither could Marissa stand the marriage. They decided in the end that going their separate ways was the only way they could deal with the situation.

Of course they never wished to divorce but it was the only way forward. As sad as it was, they each had to actually open a totally new chapter in their lives. Who would have thought and imagined this sad ending a few years back when they were still in courtship. Their marriage could not even survive the first two critical years.

**Take Home Message**

1. This story seeks to highlight, like in many marriages, the different components of a relationship that can either destroy or construct a fruitful and happy marriage. It sheds some light on how any marriage can face problems that can potentially ruin that beautiful union. Sometimes it is the small and selfish decisions that we make to accommodate our preferences that can actually destroy the love and understanding in the marriage.

2. Harbouring marital issues and living in argument can open the door of temptation and close the door of love to your spouse. There is a street term that people use for spouses who are unfaithful to their spouses, they call it **'paracetamol'**. They call it paracetamol in the sense that when you have arguments or your

spouse is treating you bad in your marriage, you start a side relationship in an effort to relieve the pain temporarily. This is what happened to Marissa, in an effort to find solace in another male's arms, she ended up developing a romantic relationship.

3. Chapter 16 of this book mainly focuses on dealing with finances in marriage. As I said love can be abundant initially, but that alone does not guarantee happiness in the marriage. If Marissa and Keith had not faced financial depression, the chance of them being together now is very high. I have seen spouses crying their hearts out because of the drastic changes in marital connection. This is quite rampant where a couple starts on a very high note but later all they have been building together can just come crumbling down as if nothing ever existed.

If we do not seek God's guidance, if we cease to work hard for our marriages, nothing can stop the devil from taking our love and happiness away.

## Tips on maintaining the LOVE environment

### Prioritise your spouse

Put your spouse first. Make your spouse feel loved and cherished through the way you conduct yourself and address them. Make her/him feel that you are still attracted to them by taking time to look lovingly at each other, little love notes or messages, run a bath for each other when time permits. Let your spouse know that your life is at its best with him or her in it, acknowledge their efforts and all the good things they do, it makes them feel important and wanted.

## Be of good cheer

I understand that we cannot be in a good mood every day and time. There is a lot of stress in life, we go through difficult times at work, with children, friends and family and it is sometimes difficult to pretend otherwise. However, maintaining a good level of happiness in the home makes for a happier marriage. Make laughter and smiles a great part of your life. Not only does it make you happy as a couple but it also helps release the endorphins that cause stress. Nobody wants to go home to a moody and hostile environment. Put an effort in cheering each other up even in distress. Maintain a marriage of smiles and laughter and enjoy yourselves while doing that.

## Be calm

According to a marriage article by Beliefnet, always be calm when approaching hot topics. Limit discussions to 10-15 minutes! Keep your voice low and calm. Use kind tones. If you find yourself getting excited, anxious or angry, STOP, take a break. Renew the discussion when you are calm again. Remember to be calm and kind as many times as you can.

## Accept each other's flaws

Understand that everybody is different in the way they behave and do things. Look at each other's flaws without passing judgement. It improves the way you approach your spouse even in the event that the flaw is getting in the way of your happiness. Try to remind yourself that everybody has flaws and find better ways of dealing with them rather than let them control your love and happiness.

## Give 110%

Go above and beyond for each other, do things for each other and show that you care. Stay up at night when your spouse is not well to check on him/her. Prepare the best meals for each other, love his/her family even if they do not really like you. Leave all you are doing to attend to them when needed. Once in a while women, watch a football game and cheer up when their team is winning even if you do not understand it. Once in a while men, pretend to be interested in watching your spouse's favourite soapies. Love and commitment is a compromise and with compromise comes peace and happiness.

# Chapter 2

# COMPLIMENTING and COMPLEMENTING EACH OTHER

It is not by coincidence that you met your husband, it is not by coincidence that you met your wife. God already knew that you were meant for each other before you even dreamt you would meet your spouse. It is not by mistake that you are married and are living with that person you call spouse.

God has given you that family as a gift, to love and to cherish despite their flaws, who does not have flaws? One of the most effective ways of keeping the bond in a marriage is complimenting your spouse. Everybody wants to feel special, treasured, wanted, valued and prioritised in life. You might not be the most romantic person who goes that extra mile to create a love environment for your spouse. Maybe you cannot do regular candlelit dinners or long weekend getaways just the two of you. You might not be all that but a compliment to your spouse does not require any financial or physical effort yet it goes a long way in making your loved one happy and feel loved.

# <u>Complimenting</u>

## <u>Dear Men</u>

Women love to feel special, yes they love to hear those sweet nothings. A compliment makes a woman softer and kinder because of the inner esteem that would have been encouraged by their spouse. Telling a woman,' I love you', 'you are beautiful' means the world and the doses are never enough. It is an expression that can be repeated a hundred times a day and still feels like it's the first time. Women yearn to hear that as many times as possible, it is reassuring to hear a husband say beautiful words.

I remember one incident when I was growing up at home, my mother bought a very nice dress and she wore it for church. On her way out, my dad was standing on the veranda and he said to my mum, 'you are looking like a member today', meaning she was looking very nice and well presentable in the society. My mum looked at him and smiled. She spend the whole day feeling very special. The best part of it was she felt so good that she bought us a lot of sweets and biscuits which was a rare occurrence. Being complimented makes one look at the world with a confident mind.

Joel Osteen mentioned in one of his seminars that, be generous with your compliments to your wife. Everyday you need to tell your spouse, I love you, I am so proud of you, I am so glad that you are in my life. They need to hear this on a regular basis not just on their birthday or anniversary. Honey it's valentine's day, 'I love you'. Once a year does not cut it, he goes on to say, if you do not tell your wife that you love her, somebody else will. Be generous when it comes to complimenting your wife.

Many women struggle with self esteem in their homes as well as in the society, because they never feel appreciated by their spouse and most of the time they end up blaming themselves for the failure to be happy in the marriage. They feel guilty and depressed because they are not made to feel adequate by their husbands. Telling your wife that you are doing a great job taking care of the house and children means a lot to any woman, it means more that an international award in their professional work.

The more you make your wife feel special, be guaranteed the more you enjoy your marriage and it also makes your children and people who surround you give you that much love and respect.

In the bible, King Solomon was considered the wisest man who has ever lived, every morning he blessed his wife. He looked her in the eyes and said, 'there are many beautiful women in the world but you excel them all'. I can imagine how the wife felt each day being praised and treasured by her husband like that, it gives a full sense of belonging. Wives can owe it to themselves to make you happy and fulfilled in the marriage. It is funny how small words can either build or destroy a marriage. Loving your wife is an investment to your entire family.

Express your love to your wife everyday without ceasing, God has made it clear that Love surpasses all understanding in 1 Corinthians 13:4-8, Love is patient, love is kind. It does not envy, it does not boast, it is not proud. It is not rude, it is not self seeking, it is not easily angered, it keeps no record of wrongs. Love does not delight in evil but rejoices in the truth. It always protects, always trusts, always hopes, and always perseveres. Love never fails.

I fell in love with the last three words, **'Love never fails'**. The focus and ultimate goal of this book is to maintain, strengthen and restore the love that married couples share. To repair where there could possibly be damage before the actual damage is done. When we follow the biblical principles of love, we realise that, it surfaces all the good things that all humans yearn for.

We may be tempted at some point to think that love can be bought through gifts, presents and all the nice things but many people have realised that the real love lies in the heart. The small but valuable gestures like words of praise, kindness, respect and mutual consideration. One singer wrote a song which says, **'The best things in life are for free'**, God gave us the capacity to love unconditionally and the heart has no measure, you can express love everyday, anytime and it never gets tired, expire or lose value.

## Dear Women

Women rejoice in being the Queens in their homes. Women want to feel in control of their life as well as their husband's life. Women want to feel special and appreciated. Yes, women we desire all this but you can never be the Queen if we do not make your husband the King.

Making your husband feel special is not a weakness. Making him feel that he is the head of the house as the bible says does not make you less important in the home. Many wives are a bit apprehensive on the term **'submission'** to their husbands. It comes off as if the wife does not have a say in the marriage. They cannot make any decisions, he always has to have the last word. Submission means a lot more than just saying okay to everything that your husband says, it means speaking your mind with respect and consideration, it means putting your heads together in making decisions in the home.

There is no happy home that can run without agreeing on important decisions. It is not a one man's journey, we all have to pull in our weight to make it work. We are so important in the family women, we should never think that we are less important. When my mother passed in 2009, after a year my father could not cope, his health deteriorated, his drive for life was shattered, he literally lost all sense of living.

We hire people to live with him and help him around the farm but he is not satisfied. With no doubt, the touch of things went from 120% to 50% for him even though the people we hire work very hard. He even mentioned that he feels like a very important part of his body has been removed painfully from him and is unable to function properly.

A home without a woman does not feel as warm as the one with a woman, so always applaud yourselves for the incredible job you are doing.

Respect your husbands, one thing that men yearn for is respect from their wives, it sets a very high bar in the marriage. When you talk to your husband, the approach and the tone of your voice must carry respect. I understand that sometimes you feel so wronged that you lose your mind as well as your humble tone of voice.

My friend was telling me that she uses the glass of water approach when she is afraid she cannot control herself. Let us learn to think first and be objective before we speak because once words are out, it is unfortunate you cannot retrieve them and they may linger in your husband's mind for the rest of his life. A wise woman talks politely to their husbands.

Be proud of your husband. Telling your husband that you are so proud of them for waking up early to go to work for the family, for the love, the support and all the positive things that they do makes them feel special and the need to do more. I was talking to a young married lady and she was telling me that, 'my husband is so difficult to show love, I do a lot of things but I do not get any response'.

It hurts for anyone to show so much love and attention but get a mute in return, however it depends on what is important to you. Sometimes it is very difficult for some men to show love, there are many reasons that surround very cold men, it can be that they never received love growing up or they simply do not understand it. People have different love languages, study what your men's love language is and continue to do good. Continue to praise him for all the good things he does, good deeds will always reap satisfactory results.

Focus on his good qualities, every human being on earth has their negatives, flaws and weaknesses, that is what life is all about. Putting all your energy and focus on your husband's flaws does not always constitute to a solution or happiness in the marriage.

Desist from living your married life looking at what he does wrong and go on and on about it forever. Remember you are investing in your life and happiness and if you decide to put so much effort on the negative, you will definitely reap negativity for the rest of your life. When you choose to be happy, it means you have chosen to deal with bad issues and move on without running your marriage on the negatives.

Most successful couples practise the, '**positive reminder approach**' (my own term), whereby you write down your spouse's positives versus the negatives, in most cases the positives outweigh the negatives. So whenever one of the spouses makes a mistake, they go back to the positive list and remind themselves of the good things that their spouse does. Also on the list of negatives, after a certain period of time say six months, if your spouse has not committed the same offence you rule that one off and reduce the negatives list. Equally, if he improves on the way he cares for you, then increase the positive list.

## <u>Complementing Each Other</u>

Complementing each other does not mean having the same interests, same appetite, same sense of fashion, same jobs. It does not mean any of these, it means living together happily despite the differences.

I think most of us have witnessed marriages where the husband or the wife is way older than their spouse. We have seen very rich people marrying average spouses. We have seen physically fat people marrying very thin and trim spouses, and we have seen interracial, intercultural and interdenominational marriages. All these unions are not by any chance a mistake. For two people to come together and agree to spend the rest of their lives together means more than what we may look at from the outside. It means there is a level of mutual understanding, feeling and connection.

For a couple to complement each other, it takes faith in each other and the main goal in the marital unity which is love. When love is present, the heart knows no boundaries, it understands all languages, races and differences. Complementing each other is not perfection but the patience you exhibit when your spouse is not in sync with you.

You sometimes wonder how certain people have managed to sustain their marriages even though they may not in our naked worldly eye seem like they are a match. I have listened at weddings and gatherings how people try to analyse whether the couple is really fit for each other based on looks or financial standing which is a shallow thing to even entertain in our minds. Surprisingly in most cases you find that these couples who do not seem to be really fit for each other actually sustain an even happier marriage and grow old together. Therefore for a couple to complement each other, it needs to come from within not on the surface.

# Chapter 3

# COMMUNICATION

As we tackle one of the most important cornerstones that constitutes a good and happy marriage. Let us be reminded that there is no and will never be a perfect marriage. It is how you decide to manage and focus your energy that determines fruition and happiness. The value that you give to your marriage matters when dealing with challenges. Let us also understand and accept that we are all different human beings, created and moulded differently. Our thoughts, decisions, preferences, likes will never be the same.

## Talk to Me

We might have heard about the importance of communication in marriage from many different sources: books, seminars and workshops. We have heard and read that communication is a fundamental key to any kind of relationship especially marriage. The question that always pop up is, 'Is it an easy thing to actually communicate in marriage', does it always work and what is the best way to communicate?' You can look into your marriage and realise that each time you try to communicate, you never succeed in whatever it is you are trying to communicate.

Many things happen in a marriage and as I have highlighted in the introduction we are different in many ways such that when we share our space, finances, love, children and all other things, it is inevitable to cross each other's paths consciously or unconsciously.

There are certain habits or interests that might not be of the other spouse's preference for example when I am driving in the car, I want the volume of the music very high for me to feel the effect of the music. On the other hand my husband likes his music low, soft and sweet. Many times he has told me that each time he starts the car, the music is so high that he worries I might have hearing problems later in life.

I have tried to listen and put the music on low but I don't enjoy the music that way, so I would rather switch off the music and create a line of thought when driving.

So in a situation where you do not believe or have the same preference as your spouse. It is important to discuss how you can compromise and deal with it because it can potentially pose friction dependant on how each spouse decides to approach the challenge. It is in most cases the way spouses approach each other that either sets the tone of compromise and understanding or hurt and offending the other.

I met a man in a bus whose marriage had just come to an end. He was drunk and he randomly spoke about why his marriage did not work. One thing he constantly mentioned was, 'We would have been together if she could only understand me for a minute, if she could have only given me the chance to speak my mind'. It was clear that what he wanted was to be heard, he desired to have been listened to. In my mind I just imagined how most of us try so hard to be right and to have the final word in an argument or misunderstanding.

I was listening to Joel Osteen on recognising what battles to fight, not every battle is worth fighting,' ask yourself, 'even if I win this battle what is the price going to be, what is the fight going to accomplish'. Unfortunately because of the ego and pride in us, we can not let an argument pass without us making a lasting statement which in most cases further escalates the situation.

Most spouses find themselves in a web of argument as a tool to solve their marital problems. I would like to highlight that when we use argument to address issues, we are literally doubling the problem because arguing is a problem in itself that also needs to be addressed. Therefore the more we tend to use argument the more challenges we have on the plate to solve.

I have used, 'Talk to me', as a sub-topic because I want us to talk about issues that affect us in reaching our utmost potential in maintaining happiness in our marriages.

So, your spouse has just made a statement that implies you are not doing a good job in your marital duties. It could be the intimacy department, housekeeping, personal grooming, handling the in laws or parenting whatever it can be. Nobody wants to feel unappreciated, you feel bitter and offended about it. Now the question is, how do you address this without making the situation worse if it is affecting you?

Below are different types of communication that enable and encourage better problem solving:

## Types/ways of Communication

> **Dialogue** - Communication is essential in good times and in bad times. When things are going well, telling your spouse how important and good they are including pointing out peculiar gestures or conduct that they have done well makes your spouse feel valued and wanted.

When things have fallen apart or you have grievances, anger, something you need clarity on. Creating a special time to talk about it is very important. I do understand that sometimes you cannot hold your grievances for long and you cannot create that sit down for a conversation time. However if your focus is to make your marriage happy, making that effort to sit down and talk about issues affecting your marriage is very important.

Dialogue reduces impromptu words that can possibly hurt one another and further escalate arguments. It strengthens the bond within the marriage, and dialogue creates maturity in your union. When you both consent to sit down and talk then your marriage is worth a great applause.

Most couples who solve their issues through dialogue tend to have more happy and fulfilling marriages than couples who are impulsive to each other.

> **Put It in Writing-** So you have tried the dialogue approach and it has always ended in a heated argument or worse. Not everyone has the capability to maintain calm when something is not going right, not everyone has the confidence to hold a sensitive conversation, not everyone has the patience.

There are many couples who can express themselves better in writing than talking. This is where spouses can write emails, letters, notes highlighting their concerns and how they can try to work towards bettering themselves. Of course it is difficult to measure the success rate of written communication but it is better than not communicating at all. It also enables spouses to open up their hearts on paper without being interrupted.

One of my long time good and bosom friend was going through a difficult time in her marriage. Her husband was always angry and could rarely show love to her. Each time they sat on the table for meals, their conversations would always end in a heated argument for no apparent reason. He did not enjoy seeing my friend happy. He always instigated petty issues to start an argument.

One day, my friend felt she had had enough even though she loved her husband dearly and wanted their marriage to work. She gathered the courage to tell the husband that she was not going to live in such an unhappy marriage, she deserved none of that. The husband started to cry and he stayed up most of the night writing a very long letter to my friend.

The letter stated that, he was a troubled man and had a lot of anger inside due to his upbringing. That was why he would always express his anger by making other people's life miserable including that of his wife and people who loved him. In the letter he also highlighted how he feels bad doing it and that he would be willing to get help from a professional if that could salvage their marriage.

The idea of putting this in writing was because he always found it difficult to share that face to face without shedding tears or ending up exhibiting anger to his spouse. By him writing the letter, it helped release some of that bottled anger he harboured for a very long time. After getting some help, even though they still face challenges here and there in their marriage, the main problem that had threatened their marriage was dealt with and now they have forged better communication with each other.

> **Third Party-** A third party in the form of a marriage counsellor, therapist, church pastors or elders is sometimes necessary in a situation where any other way of communication has failed. When spouses fail to reach a compromise or common ground when dealing with their marital challenges. We often hear that, you do not air your dirty laundry in public with regards to what happens in your marriage. Yes that serves if the laundry is aired to any person who might not be in good capacity to bring peace in the marriage. It is therefore quite pertinent that a couple agrees on who they can possibly consult to come in between and assist them.

Remember bottling up grief is toxic and unhealthy to any kind of relationship, more so that of a husband and wife, it is however very important that you know who to consult as just consulting anyone for the sake of it might create more problems. Counsellors, therapists, church pastors or trusted relatives usually have experience working with married couples and they also understand the importance of confidentiality

> **Action-** Silent treatment for example is a tool mostly used by couples to communicate their unhappiness about something. In some cases the silence can even take up to days or weeks or more. They say, 'Action speaks louder than

words'. Many marriages are run by action, the way couples behave towards each other says more than the words. Sometimes when you are dealing with challenges, there are spouses who are quick to correct their mistakes by doing the right thing without the need to talk about it or address it any other way.

This also brings the issue of understanding your spouse's love language. I have a friend whose husband always buys her gifts when he is sorry or wants to correct his mistake as a way of showing his continued love to her. We ended up making fun out of it by saying that he must continue to make mistakes everyday so that she receives more presents. By en large, action is the ultimate gesture that we want to see as a way of showing that there is progress in the relationship. It shows understanding and the will to change for the better.

Example, if you had a problem speaking with calmness each time something goes wrong. If you made everybody miserable because you are angry and not happy. Then after addressing it, you start to be considerate and talk with more care and love to your spouse means your action is showing change. You do not necessarily have to always say things because doing is more tangible.

## Rules of communication

Our main biblical principle is, 'a gentle answer turns away wrath, but a harsh word stirs up anger', Proverbs 15:1

> ➢ Never talk whilst you are still angry. Give time for you to analyse the situation because sometimes the way we perceive statements at initial conduct may not be the way it was supposed to come out or sound. Take ten sips of water or remove yourself from the situation. Take a little walk to digest if you cannot contain your anger, it has helped many.

> ➢ Listening is a skill, prioritise listening to your spouse, giving each other a chance to say what affects them is essential. You might be gifted in talking nonstop but you can never solve an issue if only one side is heard.

> ➢ Find a conducive environment that you both feel comfortable. Never in front of children or friends. The bedroom is not always the best place to do your problem solving verbally. However when you have children around, it might be convenient in the absence of a better environment to do the talk. I have seen that taking a walk or sit in the park just the two of you to discuss your issues has a better effect.

➢ Only the two of you unless you involve a marriage counsellor or therapist.

➢ Constantly remind yourself of the fruits of maintaining harmony in marriage. Life is too short. You better live two days of peace and harmony than a hundred years of misery, bitterness and grief.

➢ Remember love and God conquers all, pray about your challenges before you sit down and talk about them and remember the first day you set eyes on each other.

## Real Life Story: (pseudo names used)

## At the Verge of Divorce

Ricky and Janet received me in their modest home with smiles and a lot of happiness showing in their eyes. When I contacted this couple, asking if they could be willing to relate their marital journey for my book. They gave me a long pause and after a few seconds of anticipation, they told me that they would not under normal circumstances feel comfortable relating their story, but they felt if their story could make a positive impact to other couples out there, then they are more than happy to do so. I felt relieved and I counted down the days to meet this beautiful couple because inside, I had felt their story would inspire many couples who might be at the verge of parting ways.

Ricky and Janet had been married for over sixteen years. They had met while Janet was on college work placement where Ricky was a permanent staff and Janet a student doing her second year in Pharmacology. They said, it was not necessarily love at first sight but they felt a profound connection to each other to the extent that when Janet was off placement, he would feel her absence and how he felt happy to see her smile every day. On the other hand Janet enjoyed the attention Ricky gave her. He would take her out for lunch and just chatting with her whenever there was an opportunity. Over time they developed more than a colleague or friend feeling and they decided to take their friendship further, the rest is history.

When Ricky and Janet got married, as expected, they had two children and they presented a very happy and perfect couple so in love and focused on family. Overtime after six years, when you normally expect couples to have settled and focusing on bringing up a family, Ricky and Janet started to have problems in their marriage.

Without them noticing, they realised that each of them was pulling the blanket to their side, the quarrels became more frequent. Almost every discussion they had would end up in a big argument. Janet was getting annoyed at every small thing that Ricky did like leaving his socks in the lounge or not taking his plate to the sink and this annoyed Janet.

On one hand, Janet felt a lot of pressure with the house responsibilities, going to work, making sure the children were well catered for, keeping the house tidy, cooking and all you can think of. She felt Ricky was not doing much to help her run the house yet they were both working.

Ricky felt Janet was not a good communicator and her tone of voice was always high to the extent that it reminded him of how ill treated he was by his step mother growing up. He felt his needs were not adequately met because Janet was always tired and intimacy suddenly became a thing of the past.

From Ricky's words he said, 'I felt I was experiencing hell on earth', and Janet also felt, she deserved better in life than this kind of man. The bickering went on for another year because they felt for the sake of children they could try to just live together even though practically they were no longer having feelings for each other.

The final blow came when Janet discovered that Ricky was having an affair with another woman, apparently her long time friend. The news broke her heart as expected. She realised this had actually become a case that she never thought and felt she would be involved in.

Yes Ricky confirmed that he had an affair because each time he spend time with this lady, he felt valued and it helped him forget the misery he was living at home. He said, 'as much as I wanted and loved my family, I was not happy and did not know how to solve the problem and could not easily identify the problem either'. He obviously admitted that he felt he somehow left all the family responsibilities to the wife but he had no idea how to deal with it.

Janet said, it felt like the home that we once cherished together had become a war zone. She mentioned how she even hated his voice and how she moved all his clothes to the spare bedroom.

In all this chaos, one day Ricky had gone out on a weekend supposedly with friends. Janet took their child to a friend's and she went back home and sat looking at the mirror and said, 'God, what have I done wrong to deserve this unhappiness, loneliness and grief'. She took time to pray for herself to feel better, after the prayer, she said, 'I felt I needed to do something urgent to save my marriage, to save my family and I am starting now'.

Janet cleaned her house, packed everything, bathed and wore a beautiful dress. She mentioned that she felt good about herself for the first time in a long while. She made her husband's favourite dinner, lit scented candles and called her husband saying there was an emergency at home. He should come at once. Ricky got home breathing heavily thinking maybe something had happened to their children.

When he got home, he was welcomed by a comfortable scented home, in his words, 'I thought maybe she had a hidden agenda because this was a rare occurrence', 'but I felt at home for the first time in a long while'. Over dinner Janet spoke with calmness and love in her words. She said, 'I said a lot of things with love but deep down I was hurting'. She was asking herself why he had hurt me so much, but the will to change her marriage for the better kept telling her to try even harder.

The second day they carried on with their usual schedule and for a change she did not complain about anything. She did her things quietly and each time Ricky left his plate, she would pick it and place it in the kitchen even the socks and all other usual domestic annoyances.

Two days passed, Janet continued to do things without complaining, she was smiling and talking about other issues, watched news and made popcorn for them while watching the TV. In the evening of the third day, Janet said, Ricky approached me and said, 'My dear wife, what do you want me to do for you and how do you want me to help you?' Janet felt a strong feeling of humbleness in her and she told him, she would really appreciate if he could put his things in order, if he could help prepare the kids for bed and most of all just love her and appreciate her. Ricky felt a deep pain in his heart realising that all that he needed to do was to avoid leaving his shoes and socks in the lounge, help with the kids and just to appreciate all that Janet was doing for the family.

In awe, they looked at each other and had the longest embrace upon realising how small issues had come between their marriage and took over. Small petty issues that they could have dealt with a long while. And to think it only took three courageous days to turn the whole situation around is amazing and evokes a lot of emotion.

Ricky apologised for all the hurt he had caused her wife sometimes knowingly and sometimes unconsciously and Janet apologised for not communicating her needs in a more considerate manner.

In retrospect, they thank God for giving them another chance to work on their marriage. They have lived a marriage bliss ever since and are looking forward to aging together.

## Chapter 4

## RESPECT

Respect means being considerate, giving and showing value to your spouse. The way you talk, treat and conduct yourself around your spouse determines your level of respect to them. Everybody in the whole world needs and deserves respect, showing respect does not mean you are weak or that you are less important than the other person, it shows you are well cultured and considers the other person as equal.

According to an article published by Centre for Family Change, mutual respect means that you treat your spouse in a thoughtful and courteous way. It means that you avoid treating each other in rude and disrespectful ways e.g you do not engage in name calling, and do not insult or demean your spouse. It also means you do not talk sarcastically to, or ignore or avoid your spouse. Further it means that you view the opinions, wishes and values of your spouse as worthy of serious consideration.

It is not enough to just say, 'I respect you', the act of respect needs to take centre stage. Married couples today face a lot of challenge in showing and receiving respect from each other. It is mainly due to the different understanding and perception of respect. When couples do not understand how each one expects to be respected, then it becomes a fight of needs that are not met.

The man may consider being respected if the wife cooks, washes and run his bath. The man may consider themselves respected when a woman shows them their pay slip every single month even if they already know how much they earn. On the other hand, women may consider themselves respected if their husband takes his plate to the kitchen, helps out with chores in the house, talk to them kindly.

All these are needs that should be met through respect from each other. We looked at communication in the previous chapter, and how it is important to communicate your wants and needs with a lot of clarity to your spouse. Once again we are created different and we perceive and do things differently.

Looking back to the 50s 60s 70s, many marriages survived because they say during that time, there was more respect mainly from the women to men, and however stereotypically the respect was one sided. Mostly the women were the ones who were expected to bow down and show more respect to the men and studies have shown that this trend is still there though subtle. Men could have extra marital affairs and the women were expected to just keep quiet and accept the situation. This was mainly enforced by the family and the society in general.

Nowadays the percentage of women getting more and more independent and achieving equal goals as men has gone up. This has eventually given women more exposure to other things in the world than before. This has automatically diverted the focus from just being housewives and child bearers to being working and high achieving women. In the 1960s and before, a woman who was found cheating on her husband was shunned and taken back to her parents. It was also a very rare occurrence but in today's world we witness the liberty in women that has reduced the fear of engaging in extra marital affairs even in churches.

Respect is another cornerstone in a marriage that is very important, to the extent that the absence of it creates distance between a couple's love, connection and bond. It should come from both parties, it is not one sided.

Our marriage officer said, ' respect is like a bank account in which you deposit and withdraw money and if you are always withdrawing without making any deposits, then the account will go into negative, it becomes empty'. Love and respect work together, whenever there is respect, the love is present. It is the love within individuals that drives spouses into respecting each other.

## How to show respect to each other

1. Accept the fact that we all make mistakes and be willing to forgive your spouse for their flaws. Do not let your differences stop you from showing respect to your spouse.

2. Never take your spouse for granted, show that you are concerned about their welfare. I was attending a marriage seminar four to five years ago, one of the speakers gave an example that the first year that couples get married, if the spouse says, ' I have a headache', the other spouse runs around and even calls the ambulance for their spouse to be attended to as quickly as possible. There is the abundance of affection, kisses and hugs a downpour.

   Two years after marriage, the spouse complains of a headache, the other takes a deep breath and asks, 'have you taken anything for it'? Then five years later, the same happens, the answer will be, 'oh your cough is affecting everyone in the house now'. This clearly shows that in the course of marriage, the level of concern and sense of urgency kind of reduces and many couples end up taking each other for granted. It is very normal to go through these phases, however if you let the sleeping dogs lie, you might realise that it may be too late to awaken that fire again.

3. Talk with calmness and consideration even if the talk is not as pleasant. Shouting at each other is a sign of disrespect. Imagine if the President or Queen was to come to your house and they make a mistake, would you shout at them? If you would not, then treat your spouse like the President or the Queen. There is a saying that goes, when people shout at each other even in close proximity, it means they are faraway from each other in the heart so they shout to be heard and to be recognised.

4. Pray for each other. Nancy Van pelt stated in one of her marriage books that, it is important that couples pray for each other outside the normal family prayers. This is a special prayer channelled at your relationship, your connection, intimacy, sex life and more personal matters. Prayer is one other intimate activity that couples get involved in.

5. Listen when your spouse is talking. Show that you care about what they have to say. My husband loves to talk about politics and football,

and these two are unfortunately not my strong interests. Whenever he starts talking about these two issues, he is so passionate that each time I try to respond and contribute ideas, he can go for hours talking about it. So now when the conversation takes the route of politics or football. I really have to show that I am not bothered by not listening/paying attention. However with time, I realised I also have topics that are of less interest to my husband but when I talk I kind of expect him to pay attention even though he might not contribute. From then I realised that you feel respected when listened to.

6. Three magic words: 'Please', 'Thank you', 'I am sorry', they are simple and short words but very important words. Try to apply these words always, they work wonders. Sometimes we find ourselves so used to each other that we do not feel the urgent need to actually address our spouses using the three magic words. We feel that they already know that I am pleading or I am sorry or I am saying thank you. There are certain gestures and words that should never fade in any human being's life, and that is the three magic words. In other words I can say, address your spouse the very same way you wish to be addressed, they say, do unto others as you wish them to do unto you.

7. Accept the fact that you are different and work towards making each other happy and compromise. Scientifically, unlike charges attract and like charges repel, yes this is quite applicable in marriage too. Acknowledging and accepting that you are different from your spouse in many different ways is a tool that enables you to move forward knowing that your differences do not stop you from showing love and respect to each other.

8. Focus more on your spouse's positives than negatives. There is one approach that is constantly used by psychologists and marriage counsellors when spouses face marital problems which can threaten their marriage. It requires each spouse to write a list of the good things about their spouse and a list of the bad things about their spouse, if the good outweighs the bad then the relationship is most likely to succeed and if the bad outweighs the good then it still can be workable but more work to revamp the relationship is required.

Many times when our spouses do us wrong, we find ourselves only focusing on that particular bad incident, the negative and the worst. In most cases that ends up covering even the good things that they might have done. Of course it is difficult to see good while you are hurting and grieving but it is also pertinent to quickly deal with the negative and focus on the positive. My husband and I constantly talk about the importance of living and cherishing every moment even if we face a challenge. We always try to quickly talk it over and become happy again, and brethren we are not guaranteed of tomorrow therefore wasting too much time focusing on the negative and being unhappy is not fair to your life.

9.  Refrain from making condescending statements about your spouse to family, friends or in front of other people, like he/she is so untidy, please help her/him'. Learn to speak highly of your spouse. It does not mean the absence of challenges but it shows you respect and love each other which is most important. You are there to cheer each other even if the world cannot cheer you but you have each other to give you that confidence and recognition.

10. Romans 12:16-18, Live in harmony with one another. Do not be haughty, but associate with the lowly. Never be wise in your own sight. Repay no one evil for evil, but give thought to do what is honourable in the sight of all. A harmonious home makes you smile all the time.

# Chapter 5

# INVESTING QUALITY TIME WITH YOUR SPOUSE

## Make Time for your spouse

With the whirlwind lifestyle in the modern global community, it has left families with no time to spare for each other. Children, work, school and more seem to have taken centre stage in most homes and marriages. Creating time for each other means you still care and find each other still valuable and attractive in your life. It strengthens the bond between a couple.

I was chatting to a friend the other day and she told me that because of the shift pattern and the cost of child care, she and her husband meet each other at the door. Literally the only thing they talk about is how the children were and what needs to be attended to. They only get time with each other sometimes once a week or never at all for a month, the routine becomes so monotonous, and by the time they get home they are so tired, the only thing in mind is sleep and getting some rest.

This challenge is mostly faced by couples in the first world countries and it is always hard to juggle everything. It requires a couple to sit down and come up with a strategy on how best to make time for each other even when there are kids around. It is very easy to get into a routine of work, sleep, kids and other things that seem easier to do. The bond between couples tends to weaken the more you spend time apart without proper time to talk and laugh and do things together.

I was giving premarital advice to a young lady who was preparing for her wedding. One of the things I strongly emphasised on was to create quality time together even though it may seem impossible sometimes. I highlighted the importance of knowing that tomorrow might not come, the proper time when you are both energetic and happy to spend quality time might never come. It is therefore pertinent amidst the hectic lifestyle to set time even an hour to fully engage with your spouse and focus on nothing else.

The most important thing is the willingness to actually spend time with your spouse, this is a great starting point. Sometimes your spouse might not hold the very same passion and drive, but it is pertinent to at least put it as priority in the mind.

I have seen spouses going the extra mile. Booking a surprise weekend away, dinner for two with candles, bed covered with rose petals and all other sweet things couples do to add the spark but the other spouse fails to get it or to even appreciate all that effort. This can immensely water down many spouses' eagerness and willingness to spend that quality time with their spouse.

Spending a little money to spoil yourselves once in a while does not break the bank neither does it stop you from doing more important things like purchasing or building a house. Consider that this is not an ongoing expense and after all it is worth it. Also you do not always need the money to create quality time with each other anyway. I grew up in a farm surrounded by beautiful forests and mountains, of course I never really used to appreciate that beauty growing up maybe because it was just there in front of me and I thought real life was in the towns, oh how wrong was I.

Now when we were looking for a land to build a house, we looked at areas outside the town where there is more peace and tranquillity. I always tell my husband how I wish to live in an environment similar to where I grew up because romantic settings are a stone throw away, no need to do a budget to go for a picnic or a nice walk with my spouse.

It is very important to make use of our surrounding areas that can offer a good environment for couples without the need to pay for it.

## Tips for creating quality time together

1. Constantly remind yourself that besides all the pressure of parenting, work, chores, there is a more important person that needs attention and that is your spouse. This is every married person's responsibility to have a positive look at the importance of spending time together. It should not be one sided. I have met people who think, it is a man's job to create quality time for his wife but it surely is a wrong mentality for anyone to think that the other person is responsible for creating quality memories when you live together.

2. Plan your diaries together and take your leave days at the same time, work around making more time for yourselves.

3. Find a weekend that you can send the kids to granny's, trusted friends or arrange for a child minder and just relax the two of you. Go to church or couple's retreats. My husband and I really enjoy going on retreats and holidays together. It is a time where we can only focus on our marriage without any work interruptions.

4. Set up constant date nights weekly or monthly like Massage Nights. Most couples who create quality time for each other present a long happy marriage. The more date nights you have, the better. Remember doing date nights does not mean going out for dinner or spending money, cooking a favourite meal and candles can go a long way.

5. Find the same or similar interests, I know men love soccer and women are more friendly to soapies which creates a conflict of interest. However there are many other things and activities which you may find a common ground in, for example, taking a walk in the park or neighbourhood, window shopping in town, shopping. You can also exercise together and encourage each other by mentioning how great their body looks after sometime of working out together. Believe me everybody wants to hear that, it rejuvenates the passion and drive in continuing to do the activity.

6. Let go of tasks that are not urgent or very important. Tasks that do not change anything like watching your favourite TV programme. If your spouse suggests another activity that involves the both of you then please, TV programmes are not as important as giving your spouse that undivided attention. It might prove difficult I know, I love watching The Real

Housewives and when that programme is on, I need my space to concentrate because after watching I feel so relaxed and rejuvenated. So I used not to pay much attention to my husband when he came up with another activity to do while I watch my favourite programme, but I later realised that it was unfair to him then I resorted to recording my favourite programmes so that I can watch when I have time to myself. I did not wish for my husband to feel less important than the Real Housewives.

A relationship is like a rose, a very beautiful thing that everyone loves to have but to actually get to where the rose is, you have to go through pricky thorns. Treat your marriage as a precious gift, a gift which requires a lot of hard work and patience inorder to fully enjoy it.

# Chapter 6

# THE PAST

## The past 1

## Bury The Past

Some years ago, you found messages that your husband or your wife was writing to their ex with so much love and care just after you got married. You found out your spouse has been sending money to his/her family without your knowledge. Your spouse was bad mouthing you with their family and friends. He/she was not there when you needed them most. Of course it is hurtful and disappointing. The most difficult situation for a spouse to get over is grief and hurt caused by their spouse nomatter how far behind that happened.

When all this has happened, you may have talked about it and came to a consensus that it will never happen again and you are both willing and ready to move forward. Yes you forgave each other and agreed to open a new page. A few years, months, weeks or days pass, your spouse makes another mistake which might be similar or totally different from the previous ones. Many of us because of the anger, we get so tempted to rehash on the past mistakes to the extent that we actually overlook the current problem.

As much as we feel the need to remind our spouse of their history of mistakes. We would have taken ten steps forward but still allowing ourselves to go fifteen steps back. I have given this example in my first book on parenting where I quoted Joel Osteen where he wrote, 'some banks operate a two door system, when you open the first door, you wait until it closes behind you, only then the door infront can open to give you access to the bank. If the door behind you does not close, the front door cannot open so you become stuck or the only way is to go backwards.

We hold on to the past so much that we hinder our own happiness, progress and fulfilment in life. The past belongs **'There'** in the past, allowing your mind and self to catch up with the past is allowing yourself to be miserable. The fact that we can never go back to be in our mother's womb is a clear indication that we grow and develop, we just need to embrace new things, new challenges and new beginnings.

Always remind yourself the next time you want to rehash issues which ended some donkey years ago that, 'I am taking my happiness back twenty years ago but is it worth it?'

## <u>The Benefit of burying the Past</u>

Burying the past enables you to have a happy married life. It enables you to fulfil your dreams and cherish the presence of each other in your life. Understanding the meaning of married life is essential. I do understand that sometimes we encounter phases where our spouses do or say things that can potentially traumatise or damage our happiness seemingly forever.

Life is the way you decide to live it, when I was a teenager at church, one pastor told us a story of two couples, one couple lived in a very posh area, they had great jobs, drove the latest cars and they seemed perfect together.

The other couple was very poor, they did not even have a bed to sleep on, and they slept on a mat. The traditional African mat which is not all that comfortable, when you wake up from it, your body will be covered with traces of the mat. One thing that the pastor noticed between these two couples was, the poor couple always seemed happier. They did things together and cherished each other nomatter the circumstances. The rich couple seemed to always have issues and each time they argued, because they had a big house with spare rooms, one of them would move out of the marital bedroom to the other room.

The poor couple never contemplated so much on how poor they were and become miserable about it. Rather they were content with who they were and the love between them, they made life worthwhile. They created happiness out of unlikely situations.

So basically if you decide to hold on to issues that happened thirty years ago. You are not doing yourself a favour, neither are you solving anything but rather you are killing the life that God prepared for you to enjoy. The bible says in Isaiah 43:18-19, 'Remember not the former things, nor consider the things of the old. Behold, I am doing a new thing, now it springs forth, do you not perceive it? I will make a way in the wilderness and rivers in the desert.

## How to bury the past

**Deal with it**-Make sure when you deal with a problem, exhaust all your thoughts and emotions. One of the reasons why spouses rehash past issues is because the other party quickly apologises for doing wrong and want to move on whilst the aggrieved party is still heavy hearted. Allow your spouse to express their feelings if there is a problem. If it means crying or talking all night, then take the ride. As long as the reaction does not escalate to physical violence, long term anger or something bad. This can help your spouse to offload their grief and anger.

**Do not leave any issues unresolved**- Ensure that whenever you are angry or have a problem, speak your mind to make your spouse fully understand what you are saying and how you are feeling. Highlight the main problem as it is, how it is affecting you and how you think it can be solved. Seek professional help if you cannot get a word in edgeways. It is sad that many spouses who are aggrieved are limited on how much and what they can say because sometimes the spouse cannot stand confrontation or cannot stand listening.

## Is holding on to the past grief dearer than your happiness?

When all your bitterness is expressed and you have now decided to move on, it is pertinent that you look on the advantages of leaving the problem behind inorder to forge ahead. I always remind myself that life is too short to keep thinking about the negative, especially of the past. Your mindset determines your happiness. If you decide to hold on to past bitterness then be guaranteed of a very unhappy life. As long as changes are effected from the offending part, as long as there is no repeat of the same offence then please move on and enjoy your marriage. You are what you think and making a decision to be happy lies with you.

# The Past 2

## <u>Dealing with Bitter Upbringing</u>

Sometimes the anger that our spouses carry and exhibit is not from the day to day mistakes that we make and face in marriage. Many people have harboured anger from their childhood or growing up. They carry a heavy load of bitterness, hurt, trauma and unresolved issues. I once spoke to a very prominent person, she had achieved a lot academically and professionally. She had actually just finished her Doctorate and was setting up a research institute.

As I was talking to her, she told me that she had divorced twice because of anger issues from her side. She said her anger was so bad that each time she felt the pressure from her past experiences, she would throw anything at the husband to the extent that on one of the occasions her ex-husband suffered a terrible eye injury. She regrettably said, 'that was the end of my marriage'.

I maintained communication with her and one day when we were chatting, she mentioned that she was sexually abused by her own father as a child. She expressed a lot of emotion while relating this ordeal. Further she related how her mother and other family members did not wish to report the matter to the police when she told them after over five years of sexual abuse. The reason her family was not supportive of her claims was because the father was the main bread winner. The fear of the family not managing financially while he serves his time was more urgent for them than seeking justice for her.

She therefore clearly could not look at men in a way that is expected. She looked at men with fear and insecurity. It did not matter how well achieved she was, inside she felt empty because of what had happened to her growing up. She also mentioned how her second husband was actually very loving, caring and so kind to her, but she did not even see it because of the beast she had within.

There are men and women who do not know who their biological father is and how they look like. There are people who were ill treated because their parents had died or divorced. There are people who lived in the streets because they had nowhere else to go. There are people who were sexually abused by strangers and people who were supposed to love them.

All these experiences can trigger a lot of bottled anger from the past. There are issues that your spouse may have gone through and he/she did not or is not comfortable to disclose to you. That failure to disclose means they may be suffering inside which then comes out as impulsiveness in choices and decisions, quick to anger and even physically abusive.

## Best Way Forward

➢ Accept that the situation whatever it is happened but you are not the one who did wrong. It is someone else who God should or have dealt with.

➢ Seek forgiveness within and try to find peace within yourself. It is difficult to let go of disturbing thoughts but again your mind and heart can turn it all around. Think of the future and how best you want to live your life.

➢ Open up to someone. If you feel that you are not ready to tell your spouse about the horrible past you had, try to find someone else to open up to.

➢ Seek help. There are professionals who can help deal with cases of past grievances. Find a therapist or psychologist to take you through the steps of healing. One way or the other for the sake of your happiness, you need to get help or at least open up to someone and cry your heart out. The more you talk to someone about it, the less impact the problem will have on you.

➢ Pray about it. When you pray about something so traumatic, you offload a lot of baggage from yourself for God to deal with it. Prayer is unlimited, you can talk about your problem a million times and no one will interrupt or stop you, let alone charge you a consultation fee.

If you have gone through traumatic experiences in the past, even if you do not wish to share with your spouse, try to focus on being happy with your family. Your past does not define you, It is what comes after **'But'** that matters. You can say, 'Yes I was ill-treated growing up, **but** I am going to rise above it and be happy'. The more you have a positive outlook on life the better spouse you can be and the happier and fulfilled you can be in love and in life.

# Chapter 7

## EIGHTY TWENTY

We may have all heard about this rhetoric story of two neighbours. One of the neighbour's husband always used to open the car door for his wife whilst the other neighbour watched. In her mind I can imagine that she felt so envious that her neighbour's husband was so caring to the extent of opening the wife's car door every time. One day she mentioned to the neighbour's husband how he does a very good job opening the wife's car door every time. The husband in awe said, 'oh the reason why I open the door all the time is because the door cannot open from inside therefore the only way is to open form the outside'.

Before I talk about the Eighty Twenty. The above story is highlighting a very important aspect which affects many couples in the society. The problem of comparing their life to others, 'is my house better than theirs, do I drive the latest and most expensive car than them, do I dress up in better labels than them? The issue is who cares what car you drive, who bothers how much you earn and how you choose to use your finances?

As they say, the grass always looks greener on the other side. Many a times we undermine our own positives and spend so much time trying to be at par with other people's lifestyle. We try so much to compare our lives to others instead of focusing on our lives and our own happiness. In the process of focusing on the latter, we often end up miserable because of the time spent and wasted on not so important things. It is good to take inspiration from other couples but let us not confuse that with unhealthy competition.

When a spouse cheats, it breaks our hearts, it threatens our ego and sense of belonging. It makes us feel unloved and unworthy. The cheated party often put blame on themselves thinking their spouse has been unfaithful because they are not fully satisfying them. A lot goes around every cheated party's mind. Fear of failure in marriage, divorce, bitterness, anger. One of the things I would like to stress on this topic is, there is no reason for a married person to be unfaithful. I always believe it is way better to leave the marriage if you do not feel happy or satisfied in the marriage rather than being unfaithful to your spouse.

Many unfaithful spouses do it, not because there is no happiness in the marriage or there is a big problem in the marriage but because they want to fulfil a certain longing within them. This is what we call lust. When lust creeps in someone's mind, it tends to justify itself by seeking wrong reasons for being unfaithful, by creating a wall of blame on the other.

When married people become unfaithful, they do not always become unfaithful because they want to leave the marriage rather they do so as a form of own recreation, pass time or fun. Sometimes the spouse can do three quarters of good and and a quarter of a little weakness. The unfaithful party will go out to look for that quarter leaving the three quarters thinking they will find fulfilment but unfortunately in most cases they come out worse than they were before having an affair or being unfaithful.

From the studies carried out, it has shown that the spouses who left their marriages and went on to marry somebody else, **seventy five percent** regret the decision to have left their spouses and are willing to reconcile with their former spouses.

The message I am trying to drive home is, never feel guilty because your spouse has gone out to look for the **twenty percent**, and never blame yourself for that. Wise people try to get help and intervention in the form of therapy or church intervention when they feel burdened and unhappy in a marriage. They do not cheat on their spouses.

## What to do when your spouse has been unfaithful:

This is a very difficult topic to write or even talk about. Spouses react differently to cases of infidelity. The effects of being unfaithful are quite enormous and destructive to any marriage. There are a lot of chronic illnesses that can be caused by having extra marital affairs/adultery. Children who also suffer long term because a parent has been unfaithful, the change and dysfunction in the family union.

Ultimately the decision on how best to tackle an unfaithful spouse is entirely dependent on the aggrieved party and how best they wish to handle it. The bible says in Proverbs 6:32, He who commits adultery lacks sense, he who does it destroys himself.

1. Have dialogue with your spouse and discuss the issue including the way forward in your marriage. Ascertain that you highlight how important it is that you define your marriage and all which is unacceptable in it. Remember marriage was made Holy by God and part of respecting each other is to desist from engaging with other women or men outside of your marriage. Therefore it is God's will that married couples live within the biblical principles. Never compromise your stance with regard to

unfaithfulness. There is no reason whatsoever that can make a spouse commit adultery if not for lust.

2. **Never lose your confidence**- No human being is worth losing your self esteem for. Yes it is easier said than done because discovering that your spouse has actually decided to find someone else to share love and intimacy with is not an easy or simple thing for anyone to deal with without feeling bad about it in many different ways. However dwelling on it and allowing misery in your life does not change the situation either. Continue to wake up with a smile, look good and do what fulfils you and make you happy.

3. **Keep yourself occupied**- Always find time to do what you find joy and interest in, be it hobbies, going for coffee or tea with a friend, watch a movie e.t.c. Continue to live your life, realising that your spouse has been unfaithful does not stop the clock. The more you keep yourself busy and occupied, the more you distract bitter thoughts.

4. **Talk to God**- Prayer can change and turn your life around, God has the power to make everything right if you trust and talk to him. He has the power to guide you in the right path.

5. **Try to forgive-** Forgiving does not mean you have accepted and are fine that your spouse has cheated on you. It means you can liberate yourself from any harm that can be caused by the heartache and the disappointment.

6. **Follow your heart-** Listen to what your inner self is telling you to do. Shut your ears from what the society says and thinks. Never let the society dictate your decisions, you are the one who matters in your life. If you decide to forgive and continue in the marriage, then let it be and if you decide to move on, again let it be. It is for your own good. Never regret a decision that you made from the heart.

7. **Intervention-** Seek the help of a professional therapist who deals with marital issues if you feel you cannot take it and may do something that can hurt yourself or the children. If you also have a very trusted friend of church leaders, confide in them and get support. Dealing with it on your own may be quite detrimental to your health and sanity, however be wise on who you seek support from.

8. **Decision-**Make a concrete decision on what exactly it is that you wish to be done and to be changed. If you decide to forgive then put rules in place which govern procedures in the event of either of you having extra-marital relationships.

The rules should be clear and each one has to adhere to them.

There are many spouses who decided to endure so much heartache because of the fear of what the community may say or what the family may say. Until somebody gets infected with STDs, until they realise their spouse is not turning back. Until they realise their spouse is making plans to marry somebody else then they do something about it but sometimes it will be too late. Walk out if you feel the cheating is posing too much damage to your life, remember anything that happens in a marriage can highly affect the children.

In the bible, the only other reason besides separation by death that a spouse can seek divorce is adultery. Adultery is not permitted and viewed lightly in the bible. It is the highest point of unfaithfulness in a marriage. Therefore never compromise your values and the biblical principles that gives us a guide to a fulfilling marriage without seeking lustful relationships outside marriage.

# Chapter 8

# THE MARITAL UNION AND ITS CHALLENGES

Therefore shall a man leave his father and his mother and shall cleave unto his wife and they shall be one flesh.

This bible quote gives us an understanding that God expects a married couple to be one in everything they do and share. Many marriages today are more of a partnership than oneness. The future of many has become uncertain and you see couples who are one foot in, one foot out. I often wonder the basis of such marriages.

When I got married, I was quite an independent woman. I used to run my own life, do what I desired at my own pace and time including how I spend my money and on what I would spend it on. I love nature and travelling, so I used to plan very impulsive trips with my friends and we would get into the car or bus within a few hours of deciding to go on the trip. I owed nobody an explanation or satisfaction, life was so liberal. When I got married I still wanted to run my own finances without owing an explanation to anyone.

On the other hand, my husband had a different take on that even though he had also led an equally independent life as a bachelor. He believed in a family working together inorder to achieve family goals and reinforcing the bond and future of the family.

We sat down to plan how we were to run our finances and even though inside I wanted that financial independence. I looked at the bigger picture which is, we are one flesh and working together to develop our life. I felt this was quite essential and beneficial not only financially but it would also help forge an even tighter bond. This decision clearly paid off as I realised our goals were met quicker and smoothly. It also helps when the other spouse does not have an income because your money is our money, we work with what is there.

## Challenges and Drawbacks in the Marital Union

### Competition

When a marriage is made up of two people who want to show each other that they are better than the other, then it becomes very unhealthy. Most marriages where spouses compete financially, professionally, academically or materially always end up in disastrous situations which can affect the whole family including children. It is very important to revisit the definition of marriage so that it guides your perception, in biblical terms being one flesh means you share everything. What is yours is mine and what is mine is yours. Unfortunately we have more of what is yours is mine and what is mine is mine and what is mine is mine from both parties.

It is unfortunate to be in this situation as it has the potential of breaking marriages. Infact one of the contributing factors to the high divorce rate is competing in marriage. Who cares if you earn more than your spouse, who cares if you are able to buy the latest ride? All these things do not give any happiness to marriage. It is the love you share and harmony that really counts and matter in life.

I once worked with a very young and beautiful lady who was married to a very rich husband but way older than her. She was quite open that she had married for the luxury. She wanted a hustle free, stress free and comfortable life. She believed marrying a rich man would fulfil her wishes and she would be a happy woman. Three months into the marriage she started to feel a certain emptiness, she would say, 'she had everything but something was lacking in her life which she could not point a finger to'.

Five years later she was still not completely happy. She needed more out of life. She decided to go to school and acquire an education to look for a job and create something to do. In all the hustle to find material satisfaction, she lacked love for the person she had married. The only thing she considered before getting married was being able to do whatever she wanted and live lavish. She only realised later that life is not only about material comfort but love, connection, bonding and happiness within.

When she got a job, she decided to start her life anew. She divorced the rich man and started her life with less comfort but more happiness and fulfilment.

This young lady's story is meant to stress that, material things are not worth competing for. They do not guarantee happiness at all. Therefore, the more we try to compete with our spouses in the home, the more we drift apart without necessarily noticing. Even if you build a mansion without working together, it still belongs to both of you because you are married.

**Love for power**

Similar to competition, the love for power is another contributing factor that makes couples work separately. The mentality that drives one to want control over the other in everything. It is sad that sometimes when spouses do not understand marriage well. They see it as a one sided union in which only one, has to put a stamp on family decisions and call all the shots which I think in my opinion fuels injustice and oppression.

The love for power takes the love and respect away from one's heart, power kills and deceives. A man or a woman who truly loves and cherishes their spouse understands that there is no one more powerful than the other because the bible clearly states that you are, 'one flesh' and being one means equal.

For a marriage to work better, superiority complex must never exist in the marriage. The moment a spouse feels much higher in esteem than the other, it removes 'US' from the same page. The page of love and walking together in harmony in all the things you do as a family. Many couples have ended up making destructive decisions because they wanted to have the last word and disregarded any opinion or contribution that comes from the other.

The love for power can be exhibited from both the husband and the wife's side. I have heard many people say, men have been found to be more guilty of love for power in a marriage but more and more, women have also taken that role where they feel it is their way or the highway.

## Distrust

Lack of trust always leaves a salty taste in one's mouth. As much as trust is earned overtime and is determined by what the spouse does to earn or lose it. It is quite pertinent in a marriage to build that trust. Trust controls how secure and happy you are in the marriage and our main focus is to achieve that.

Many have asked that, 'if a spouse has cheated on you and you forgive them, how possible is it to trust them again? This question is very difficult for anyone even a professional to answer. Mainly because the answer lies in one's heart and behaviour, however there are many measures you can take as a couple to account for your life.

I was talking to a couple who had just undergone a hurtful episode of unfaithfulness in their marriage. Apparently the husband had continued to communicate romantically with his ex-girlfriend after they got married for over a year. All that while, the wife was in marriage bliss and enjoying her husband and convincing herself that she was that one and only Queen of his heart and life.

By sheer mistake, the husband accidentally forgot to log off his facebook account and the wife upon tidying the house, came across all the messages that the husband and the ex girlfriend had been sending to each other. The messages carried the graphic romantic involvement that they had been experiencing behind her back, including details of their sex escapades and how they wish they could have lived together forever.

For any other normal woman or rather human being, this level of infidelity can totally push you to the wall.

The wife threatened to leave the marriage but the community, family and friends persuaded her to forgive her husband and pray hard for the marriage. She decided to give him another chance because she loved her husband and she surely wanted her marriage to work, the remaining problem was trust.

She started putting restrictions on where the husband could go without her and what time he should be home. She kept account of the time he finished work and approximate travelling time back home, any extra time required accountability. His phone and laptop became her new toys. She even demanded that he give her all the passwords to his email accounts and all outlets she suspected would enable him to communicate with women.

It became so unbearable for the husband to the extent that their relationship was becoming more of a workplace than a home. At the same time the wife needed to do those checks to guarantee trust.

One day the husband decided to talk to his wife about the whole issue. He made her aware that, it was not by keeping the passwords to his emails that would effectively stop him from communicating with other women but the conscience within his heart and respect for his marriage. He mentioned that the internet is so vast that it is easy to open another account without her knowledge. So, he assured her that he would work hard to restore the trust in their marriage again without the need for her to keep track of all his communication channels.

He expressed that he had realised and learnt from his mistake and was willing to work hard to gain her trust again and make her a happy wife.

The wife took his word but she still felt that little, 'Maybe' inside. To cut the long story short, she is still on the road to gaining trust but she has since stopped to worry so much about it.

So Trust can make or break a marriage. Lack of it can trigger many problems including suffocation caused by too much control which is not a good ingredient for a healthy marriage. The message to take home is,' Trust is earned not bought, earn yours in your marriage today and God will bless your union abundantly.'

**Family interference**

Genesis 2:24, Therefore shall a man leave his mother and father and shall cleave unto his wife, and they shall become one flesh. The bible emphasises on leaving not as a physical departure of a child going to live somewhere with someone for a while. Leaving in the context of being independent from the comfort of always consulting and seeking decisions about your life from the parents. Leaving in the capacity of being able to fully commit and dedicate your love, life and energy to your spouse.

One of the biggest challenges that marriages face today is the lack of understanding and belief in being independent from parents and other families when making big decisions and planning in their marriages. There are more cases today of spouses who divorced because they never felt valued in running their family affairs due to family involvement. I know sometimes it may be difficult for someone to easily disentangle themselves from getting approval from mum or dad in everything they do. Sometimes it is even done innocently without realising how bad it affects the spouse.

Many families struggle to let go of their children too. They always want to meddle in their married children's affairs to the extent of getting angry if decisions are made without their knowledge. The involvement of family in your marital affairs can make you lose the sense of control of your life and may end up splitting the union in planning together. These are the cases where you see the husband building his own house and the wife doing the same.

It is sad to say, situations like these do not always end well, as the bible says, therefore a man shall leave his father and mother and shall cleave unto his wife, and they shall become one flesh. It clearly shows that God's plan is for married couples to be independent from any outside interference and work together, do everything together as one. The minute you cease to work in unity, God takes the blessings from us and instead of achieving family goals sooner, we end up taking forever to achieve our goals.

It is therefore pertinent for married couples to communicate well with their extended families before getting married on the limits and boundaries they should respect in their marriage. Parents and siblings who love you will always understand and respect that your life has changed and their involvement in running your life is not needed unless consulted. This enables you and your spouse to be free and flexible in doing things together. Please get this point right, this does not mean you stop supporting your parents and families from where you came from. Continue to support them in any way you want without involving them in your family plans and let all the support be transparent to both parties.

## Unforgiveness

Not being able to forgive brings misery in any kind of relationship but more so in a marital relationship. The fact that you live under the same roof, sleep in the same sheets, share everything surely means you either choose to forgive and be happy with them or simply move on if forgiveness is beyond reach. Again a reminder, we only live once and God gave us this precious time on earth to learn enjoy and love.

As I have highlighted in the previous chapters, no human being is perfect, even in our sleep we dream horror therefore we are definitely bound to step on each other's toe. People make mistakes, so holding on to the past mistakes that your spouse committed sometime ago may strain the way you run your marriage. The more we forgive the more we can achieve positive change in our marriages, holding on to things is not the quickest way to achieve happiness in a marriage. It makes us become slaves to misery.

## Peer or external influence

It is great to have friends and family around us, we all need that. Human beings cannot live without social interaction, friends and family define us one way or the other. When we are happy, we want to share the happiness with our friends and family, when we cry, we want to cry with them. They give us the comfort and the support we all need.

Surround yourself with positive people, people who add value to your life not people who actually want to steal that value from you. Refuse to be associated with people who spend **seventy five percent** of their lives talking about other people, each time you talk about another person, ask yourself if you have sorted your life first. Make friends who teach you to be a good person to your family, friends who pray for you and pray with you when things are not going well, and friends who believe and trust in you.

One thing God made just right is the ability to choose friends. Unlike family who you can stick to whether they choose to walk the streets naked or steal or commit murder. With friends you can choose the quality or quantity you want. My advice would be the lesser closer friends you have the better. This does not mean you become unfriendly to other people but, your inner circle should consist of well vetted friends, believe me our friendships can either build us or destroy us. It is therefore very important to make wise decisions on who you choose to share your social life with.

Personally, I take time to engage with people. I always want to take my time to evaluate and study their character based on the quality of conversations and general conduct. If a person is too centred on being materialistic, opportunistic, competitive and focused on what other people do then I really struggle to forge a friendship. I have had friends in the past who have disappointed me, it is very hard to find genuine friends in this day and age.

All my life, I have met very few genuine and loving friends. They do not only bring positivity in my life but friends who actually go to the extent of fasting for three days for my life. I remember vividly one touching experience. I had just lost my mother and at the same time I was preparing for my wedding later that year and my life was so hollow. I had lost drive in everything even getting married. The wedding preparations were a nightmare, in a nutshell I was a mess because I had lost my pillar of strength and my love.

All this time I did not even tell my friend exactly what I was going through. One day amidst all this, my friend called and said,' I want us to fast for three days'. ' I want us to pray for your wedding and marriage and comfort for the loss of your mum'. Ever since I was born besides my mum, I had never heard anyone tell me that they are praying for me, let alone fasting for three days.

We prayed and God answered our prayers. From that day on, as much as I already had a high regard of her, this incident made me realise how much of a treasure and a valuable friend she was. Up until today she is the one person who tames me even when I want to make the wrong decisions. She is not a friend who tells me what I want to hear, she tells me what works and what is right.

We never spend time gossiping because we both have families and many other things to take care of in our own lives than spending time focusing on other people. In a nutshell in a marriage, we may not all find very good and faithful friends but it is important to have people who make your life develop, people who genuinely cry and laugh with you.

Somebody was telling me the other day that her husband was sweet until he started hanging out with a certain group of people who compete to buy the latest cars on loans, drink alcohol and have affairs outside their marital home. She said one day they came home and found her husband helping to change baby diapers and they told him that it was a woman's job, and because he wanted to feel macho, he succumbed to it and reduced his effort in helping the wife with the baby and other house chores.

I also know of two ladies in Mozambique. These two friends seemingly loved and cherished each other. They spend most of their free time together doing different activities together. One of the friends was married to the Director of a big parastatal. Periodically, they used to go to the traditional healer together to get potions for the husband not to stray, the other friend was not married. All this time, the unmarried friend had become envious of her friend's life to the point of wanting her husband. Little did the married friend know that her friend was not so happy because she was married to a prominent and financially stable man.

So when they returned from the traditional healer, she was given a potion to put under the husband's pillow and magic would start soon after. The friend was present so she heard how the potion was going to work. Jealousy and envy took over to the extent that she secretly approached the friend's husband and warned him to be careful with his wife. She told him that his wife wanted to kill him so that she can take all his properties. She explained to him about the potion and even advised him to go and check under the pillow for proof.

The husband in shock went and all came out as the wife's friend had said. He was so disappointed and annoyed by his wife's behaviour and decision to try and eliminate him. He ordered the wife to pack her things and leave his house. She left with the children and had to start life from scratch.

While the wife was away, her friend was busy making contact with the husband. She lured him into marrying her a few months after her friend was chased away. When the friend heard about it, she was dumbfounded and could not believe her trusted friend had betrayed her to that extent. I tell you brothers and sisters in marriage, not everyone is happy to see you happy and to see you prosper in your life as well as in your marriage. Be very careful who you bring into your life, the bible says in 1 Corinthians 15:33, do not be deceived, bad company ruins good morals. And also Proverbs 13:20, He who walks with wise men will be wise, But the companion of fools will suffer harm.

It is not wrong to draw a line on who can access your home and information in your marriage. My advice would be to find friendship in your spouse and children most than any other person.

In as much as it is important to have friends and family around us, we need to look at the quality of friends we bring into our marriages. One gift God made for us is the capability to choose friends, unlike family you cannot choose. God wants us to choose and not make a mistake of choosing fake friends who only want us because of a b c or friends who come to us for competition. Never entertain friends or family who destruct your marriage by discouraging you from doing good to your spouse, never give people like that any attention and platform.

## Future uncertainty with spouse

The scariest thing to possibly happen in a marriage is when you are in it but not completely sure whether you fully belong or are in it for the long haul or you are just testing waters. There are many different reasons why people become uncertain of their future in marriage. One, when you face problems in the marriage and your spouse always talks negative about you for example, how he thinks he has made a mistake marrying you. It weakens the grip of security from your spouse. The words you say to each other when angry can destroy what you may have built for many years.

As in the previous chapter, unfaithfulness is one major reason why most couples are uncertain of the future. Eventhough women are becoming more and more unfaithful as men in the past. The fear of waking up and finding out that your husband has decided to marry someone else is disheartening, just the thought of it. This kind of feeling hinders a lot of progress in a marriage, the love, and the children's happiness. Being at limbo in marriage is also very dangerous as it can potentially open the doors of temptation. When a spouse does not feel assured in their marriage, it means even the future is difficult to plan.

## Loneliness in marriage

You wake up one day and realise you are married but you just feel empty, abandoned and worse than when you are physically alone. It presents a great sadness to see a beautiful marriage surviving without emotional presence. Many marriages are in that state today and no one is doing anything about it.

I was talking to a young lady who had been married for six years. As she was relating the situation in her marriage, something struck me that she was so lonely, apparently lonelier than when she was as a single person.

This beautiful young lady was in love with her husband and the husband was equally in love with her. The love they shared drove them into deciding to take the next step which is getting married. They had a lovely and beautiful wedding which left everyone in envy so to speak, envy in a good way.

She went on to say, married life was so good and she felt so loved and cherished by her husband. They would spend most of their time together. They created more time together even in their busy work schedules. Each time she got dressed or had a new hairstyle, the husband would complement her and tell her how beautiful she looked, and how he was the luckiest and happiest man in the world because he had found her.

Life was so sweet, they were blessed with a baby a year after the marriage and as expected, they rejoiced in having a new addition to the family. The child brought even more joy, love and bonding to the family.

Three years down the lane, she began to notice a difference in the way they related to each other. They stopped endearing each other and calling or texting each other while at work. The usual gestures that made their bond stronger had suddenly became something of the past. She realised they could not even hold a meaningful conversation with each other without arguing or getting a cold response. She thought it was a phase which would eventually pass but inside, she felt a distance between the two of them. Even with him right next to her, she felt they were far away from each other.

For over a year they battled loneliness in the marriage. Each time they had something exciting happening in their life worth sharing with each other, they would call other family members and friends to share the news or to just wind down after a stressful day instead. They ended up spending more time with other people rather than themselves. Sadly she said, all the love she once felt a few years before had died down and she felt she could not accommodate him in her heart and he felt the same.

My big question to her was, what had made them grow apart and lose the love and passion they once felt for each other. Her answer was quite sad because she had no idea why the marriage had taken such a sour turn.

On this account, I'm driving at understanding that there can be loneliness in marriage. In life you do not necessarily become lonely because you have no one around you. You can actually be lonelier with a hundred people surrounding you. Many issues can trigger loneliness in a marriage. Boredom and lack of connection can play a big role in creating loneliness in marriage.

It is very important for married couples to constantly assess their marriages to evaluate where there is need for improvement on certain areas or even evaluate the success in the marriage. It is quite helpful for any couple to look into their marriage and identify where more attention needs to be focused.

As I have mentioned in the previous chapters, marriage is hard work and to avoid being lonely in a marriage it is necessary to put that extra effort in it. A lot of negative things happen where there is loneliness. The temptation may kick in, spouses may opt to look for happiness elsewhere as in looking for that extra marital affair just to fill the void, just to have someone to talk to and someone who can listen to them. Loneliness can easily cause depression and stress and also spouses may end up hanging out with the wrong crowd who can be a negative influence on the marriage.

Let us be reminded that God made Eve to be a help and companion for Adam because God had seen how lonely Adam was and in need of someone to share God's blessings with. It is unfortunate that today because of the constant pursuit of economic stability, spouses are more of business partners than companions. It has become more of, what bill needs to be paid, who is picking the kids from school and please help me with the dishes. It is very important to understand that marriage is not just for procreation and coming together. Marriage is for spouses to give each other company, to cheer each other up, to make each other laugh and to share their feelings and thoughts.

## Migration

Due to a high level of political and economic instability in different countries. Many families have felt the need to migrate to peaceful and economically stable countries in an effort to be able to sustain their families. In most cases one of the spouses takes the first leap before the whole family. When families decide on taking this challenge, they often feel and think the process is going to be easy but many people actually have to struggle more than they were in their troubled countries.

Different countries take on specific professions which cannot be easily filled by their nationals, for example the UK takes on more of the migrant health and social care professionals like nurses and social workers. Other professionals will definitely be quite difficult to get a professional job which can grant better residence.

When spouses struggle to get residence or work permit in a foreign land that means the family has to stay for a longer time in the other country. As a result situations like this have caused a lot of heartache because of distance and lack of enough resources. I have seen and heard cases where spouses have ended up starting new families on either side of the world which has even ended up in divorce.

If a couple is not very strong, it can be very challenging to continue to work together transparently in a long time distance marriage. Therefore many couples may find themselves working separately. It is quite difficult to even prescribe possible steps that can help to tighten the marriage bond even while residing in different countries. However, it is important to strengthen the communication line and working hard inorder to be on the same page.

## Social Media

Nowadays facebook, twitter, instagram and watsup have become more of a community. These are platforms which many can link with people who are in many other different continents. Almost everyone has become easily accessible. Social media has opened many positive and negative contributions to the marriage union. Because of social media, people have a platform where they can vent their anger or express their happiness to the world. I have seen many articles of spouses exposing their cheating partners for the whole world to know and see. Sometimes in the heat of anger, people can use many weapons as an outlet and in today's world, many have found an outlet and revenge in social media.

Many marriages have also broken and lost grip due to social media. Spouses can easily communicate with ex boyfriends and ex girlfriends or even create and start extra marital affairs.

Not only is social media causing a lot of social unrest, it is also stealing a lot of quality time that spouses should share. It seems many people find facebook updates and tweets from celebrities and other people more fascinating than spending time with their spouses.

It has proven very difficult to find a solution to reduce the time spend on social media. It is therefore up to each individual to prioritise what they find more important between spending time with family or checking updates on facebook or twitter.

# Chapter 9

# SECRET RECIPE TO A HAPPY MARRIAGE

## Be at Peace with yourself

Invest in your inner happiness and peace before you can even consider making somebody else happy. Many things may have happened to us in the past, things that make us feel miserable, unhappy and aggrieved or things may still be happening. One most important thing in life is to accept situations and move on and also putting your burdens to the Lord, he surely listens. Never bother about things that you cannot change. Certain things happen in your life to cause distraction and take your happiness away but never pay too much attention to such. God gave us life to live and cherish what he blessed us with.

I will give an example of a donkey, one day a farmer's donkey fell into a well. Terrified the donkey cried for hours as the farmer tried to find ways to rescue it. At the end the farmer decided the animal was too old and impossible to retrieve and then he thought the well needed to be filled to prevent future losses. He invited the neighbours and friends to help him fill the well with sand.

They took shovels and began to throw sand into the well. At first, the donkey realized he was being buried alive, he cried horribly. Then to everyone's shock, the donkey quieted down. A few shovels later, the farmer looked down the well and was astonished at what he saw. With each shovel of sand that hit the donkey's back, the donkey would shake it off and take a step up. As the farmer and his neighbours continued to throw dirt on top of the animal, he would shake it off and take another step. Soon everyone was amazed as the donkey stepped up over the edge of the well and happily trotted off.

In short, this story is teaching us to be brave even in the time of adversity. No matter how much sand is thrown at you, in laws not liking you and making your life hell, unemployment, people talking negatively about your marriage, continue to shake it off and step up. This is the only way you can ever make your spouse happy if you deal with your inner peace and sanity.

## Wear the cap of marriage, not the cap of knowledge

Although we get a certificate of marriage at the beginning of marriage, we never graduate in marriage. I am sorry ladies and gentlemen but academic achievements are not the cornerstones to a happy marriage. We do not require academic or professional curriculum vitae to fall in love or to get married. The illusion coupled by the ever evolving world has left spouses in want. Everyone is in constant pursuit of economical stability, professional upgrade and social status. Yes things have changed and everyone has to hold those high positions and bring a fat pay cheque home.

There is nothing wrong with all the achievements that both men and women are attaining. There is nothing wrong with a woman bringing in a very fat pay cheque, neither is there with a man running twenty companies. All that is God's blessings to humankind and we can embrace them with open arms and satisfaction. However there is a trend of feeling more powerful than the other because of these achievements. There was a trending story in the news about an immigrant man living in Canada who supposedly killed his wife because he felt threatened by her achievements. She had become a professor and he felt less of a man, less of a macho so to speak. Insecurities rise especially on the men's side if a woman is successful, it is sad to say but this is a reality in many homes and a great cause of friction.

I have also come across women who have attained success academically and professionally but cannot come to terms with the idea of submitting to their spouse because they sure feel too special to do so. I have seen good marriages break because of this.

**NOTE:**

1. Your degree or success does not make a constitution in the home. It belongs to your job, it belongs to your workplace, it belongs to your business. Continue to submit and to love as the bible says. This is for your happiness and life fulfilment

2. Enter the marital home as **'THE WIFE', 'THE HUSBAND',** not The Doctor or The Lawyer or The Teacher. Your professional titles are meant for your workplace or with friends outside the home.

3. Constantly remind yourself why you are married

4. It's good to be successful but there is nothing so peculiar about it that can make you feel too important over your spouse.

5. Remember to take off your cap of knowledge at the door of your marital home and wear the cap of **MARRIAGE.**

## Those with successful spouses

1. Reduce insecurities, studies have shown that most men become threatened by high achieving women even before they take time to know and evaluate them which creates paranoia that can make men see them as if they are being disrespectful even without any proof to show it.

2. Celebrate a successful woman/man and respect them for who they are, not what they have achieved, support their achievements.

3. Invest in the success of your wife/husband, it is not only for her/his benefit but for the children as well.

4. Look at the positives not the negatives

5. Work towards bettering yourselves even more, remember this is not a competition but you are adding more value to your family.

## Shower your Spouse with Kind words

I have always said words are so strong that they can either build or destroy a human being, words are the backbone of life, words create friendships and enemies.

I don't know if he knows but each time my husband says something sweet to me like, 'I love you' or 'you look gorgeous', I become weak to the bones such that I don't know what to say. It makes me want to cry of happiness within. Sometimes words are so therapeutic, they are a balm to the heart and soul. If we make it a habit to whisper kind and sweet words to our spouses, the likelihood of too much argument and hurting each other is very low.

Endear each other, I love to be called sweetie, honey, darling, it makes me feel good inside and out. I also enjoy endearing my husband and his eyes always tell me he enjoys it.

Kind words make a person on the receiving end kinder in the relationship.

Whenever one of us travels without the other, we always use more love and sweet words for each other. Telling each other, 'I miss you terribly', 'It's not the same here without you', makes up for the physical absence. It is like glue that sticks the two hearts together nomatter how far you maybe from each other. Be generous with words to your spouse. Tell them how they look nice in what they are wearing and how you find them so irresistible.

## Enjoy each other

Remember that day you met and you felt butterflies in the stomach. Every time you were going to meet each other, you would lose your sleep and you carefully chose what to wear and practice what to say? And when you meet, you are so nervous that you talk nonsense and behave way out of line. That feeling there meant you love him or her so much that you lose your senses.

It might not still be the same after marriage and having babies, running the house and extended families. It is tough to go back there, however nothing can stop you from celebrating and enjoying each other.

You do not need money to find enjoyment in your relationship. Always continue to look your spouse right in their eyes and stare for as long as you want, switch off all gadgets and hold each other and pat. Even when you are doing chores in the house like dishes, it is a good opportunity to be playful with each other, splash each other with soapy water, draw his or her face with flour or baking dough…I mean anything you can think of. Never let chores stop you from enjoying each moment. Tickle each other and run around the house chasing after each other even if you have twenty kids, you are still a husband and a wife.

Have fun, don't take marriage too seriously. If you feel you are putting too much effort or feel like what you are doing is more of duties than the expression of love then you need introspection.

## Show love

I have never come across a person who does not want to be loved. It is the most beautiful thing in life to feel loved especially by your spouse. It makes us smile and feel at ease even when things are not going well at work, we look forward to going home to be loved and cherished. In my five years of marriage I have realised one thing, it is more fulfilling to show love to my husband through words, gifts and sharing. I feel happy to tell my husband that you look so cute and I love you so much, he surely makes my world go round.

One of the things I love doing is making food and each time I prepare food with passion and that extra touch for my husband, it just doesn't make us eat good food but I am communicating my love to him. When we went to Zimbabwe on holiday, most of the people we visited would cook for us and one day my husband said, I really miss your food, obviously the food was good but he probably missed that touch of love and passion.

Continue to show love nomatter what, it pays off one beautiful day

## Give More, Expect Less

I know, we all want to receive love, gifts, pampering…..
everything but have we thought how fulfilling and
enjoyable it is to just give? Let us give more of our love
and time to our spouses. To actually say I am here for
you sweetheart, let's talk or lets go for a walk can mean
the world to your spouse.

Give more of those gifts you so much want, instead of
expecting, let us give. Give more of your time, gifts,
smiles and laughter. The more you rejoice in making
your spouse happy, the more your life will be more
meaningful. Imagine if for everything your spouse
gives or does to you, he expects the same in return. It
would be cumbersome and uncomfortable, also we all
have different ways of showing each other love, like the
five different love languages, it's not always one way
that gets to a spouse's heart, some enjoy words, some
gifts, some physical touch.

## Identify your spouse's love language

According to Gary Chapman, there are five main types
of love languages. Sometimes we expect our spouses to
do things a certain way but it might not be the same
way they feel. Therefore it is very important to study,
learn and know your spouse's love language so that
when he does something a certain way, it is clear to
you what message they want to convey for example,

you might expect your spouse to say sorry after he wrongs you but maybe he feel better if he buys you flowers. So instead of waiting for a sorry, the flowers would have conveyed the sorry through your spouse's love language.

1. **Words of affirmation**

   As I have highlighted in the previous chapters, the importance of complementing your spouse. Words can make or break a good family. Every time my husband says, 'I love you', there is a noble feeling I cannot explain from the inside, it feels good and it makes me feel special and loved, it sets a tone for the day. However, this might not be everyone's love language, this can mean far less to someone else even though it is very important.

2. **Gifts**

   Passing by that florist on your way home could be a noble idea, it can set the tone of love in the home. Gifts are a sign of appreciation and your spouse can feel whole through receiving or giving a gift. A gift does not always need to be expensive. The main reason for a gift is not because your spouse needs it. It is a sign that you are thinking of them all the time. If your wife or husband likes a certain type of bread or fruits, passing by his or her favourite store to get it for him/her can mean the world.

### 3. Quality time

Life has changed so much, with the constant pursuit of economic stability and trying to keep at par with the modern lifestyle. Many spouses are starved of that Quality time because there never seem to be a time when you are both energised and in tune to just sit and talk and love each other. Spending that quality time with your spouse is very important, going out to the park, taking a walk, jogging together, going for dinner or just sit in your bed and chat to each other.

### 4. Physical touch

Physical touch means you are desired. Holding hands while walking to town, intimacy, cuddling, leaning on each other can make your spouse feel your presence and that they belong.

### 5. Acts of Service

Doing things for each other, preparing a meal, run a bath, do the dishes. Men, when you take time to do the house chores, it means the world to your wife. Running to the shops last minute to get her a new lip gloss because hers has run out makes her blush.

Ladies, making pop corn for your spouse while he watches his favourite football game creates a theatrical ambient for your husband. Never cease to do things for each other.

All these love languages complement each other, however a person might not possess all these qualities, it is your duty as a spouse to know your spouse's love language, it helps you to know when he does this, it means something profound.

## Forgive Quickly

I can only say as God has forgiven us, forgiving is meant to set you free from the bondage of holding on to grief. We all are bound to err in our marriages but forgiving your spouse makes the marriage more fulfilling. When they say marriage is hard work, it is not the house chores or taking care of the children that is being referred to. It is the capability to accept your spouse's flaws and forgiving even in the most unlikely situations.

## Apologise

We teach our children to apologise every time they make a mistake. We teach them so because it is the kindest and humbling thing to do. It makes them likeable and beautiful inside. I have met quite a number of spouses who find it very difficult to apologise to their spouse when they do something wrong. Pride is the main culprit that makes people feel less important, weak or irrelevant if they apologise. However, one of the best qualities that a human being can possess is the ability to humble themselves and apologise. Apologising does not mean you are less macho or important, it means that you have a heart, considerate and enjoy making peace.

Every spouse must learn to accept where they do or go wrong. If we look at the justice system. We often hear of people who had their offences pardoned and sentences reduced because they plead guilty and took responsibility for their offence. It is a lesson to all of us, the more we accept and seek forgiveness from our spouse, the more we get to live a happy married life.

When we look in the bible, David was one of the people who was closest to God. David made a lot of mistakes in his life. He committed many sins, he committed adultery and murder but one exceptional thing that David did was that, he always accepted his mistakes and would always seek forgiveness from God. He never ceased from apologising, he never counted how many times he apologised. He understood that each time he committed a sin, it was noble for him to seek apology from the creator.

We can never apologise enough, we therefore have the responsibility to accept and apologise to our spouses.

## Increase your intimacy

The more intimate you are, the closer the bond. A marriage without intimacy is like an unseasoned meal, a meal with nothing, no salt just bland. As we look at the chapter of intimacy, people leave their parental homes to be with a husband or wife because of the intimacy they can only share with a spouse not with a brother or any relative. Intimacy in a marriage defines your relationship, the more intimate you are, the more married you are. The less intimate, the more gap you create in your marriage. The more temptation to become unfaithful. The more miserable a marriage will get. Cease to make your marriage a business. Do not just become partners in running the financial and the children's welfare. These can come as a bonus to what you already share but also give priority to your intimate life.

Explore new styles and positions of being intimate, be adventurous in the bedroom. Adam and Eve were naked and not ashamed. Be confident with your spouse during intimacy, your bodies belong to each other and that means there are no boundaries. I have a friend who got married a long time ago, she would tell me how shy she was taking off her clothes while her husband watched. So she always created a lot of things to do towards bed time so that she would find the husband already in bed so that she could just switch off the lights before taking her clothes off. It took her quite a while and a lot of encouragement from the husband for her to feel comfortable to be naked around the house with her husband.

Also adopting a culture of reading any material that focuses on marriage and intimacy can broaden your knowledge and horizons to reach during intimacy. It is quite pertinent to take the time to explore each other and connect as a husband and wife.

## Never fear your spouse

There are many marriages that are hanging by the rope right now because they are limited on what they can do or say to their spouse. Be free and be comfortable with each other to the extent that you can tell each other off without quite feeling bad or fear that your spouse will be offended. It is however important to learn a better approach when addressing your spouse.

Help each other if your spouse needs help. Let's say your spouse has developed halitosis and each time he/she opens the mouth you drift away. Would you be afraid of telling him? Never be afraid to tell your spouse that their breath is not very pleasant and help him/her find a solution, that way you can find a solution for it together. His/her problem becomes ours. I have grown to think my husband is my mirror and I am his. If I leave the house with disgusting stuff sticking on my mouth, I take it as his fault because if he has seen that, it is solely his responsibility to tell me to do something about it.

The other rampant fear experienced by spouses is the response they get if they say or do something. I have a cousin who does not appreciate discussing family problems. Each time his wife tries to address an issue that is affecting their marriage, he gets very angry to the extent of distracting the real problem. After that he becomes so moody and unapproachable for a very long time. That way, the wife can never gather the courage to even approach him again about the matter. There are many spouses who do not want to be asked if they have done something wrong, however marriages should never operate that way because it means challenges will never get to be solved.

## Communicate

Learn to just say it, nomatter how you feel, say what you think and feel. It helps your spouse to treat and handle you better. Many people stay in the boat and agonise, wish their spouse could do things differently, hope their spouse could change and listen to them even if you do not say anything. Even when it comes to making love, be open to your spouse about how and where you want to be touched and what actually brings euphoria to you during sexual intimacy.

We have to remember that life is already stressful given the economic situation today which requires an average family to work harder. There is work related stress, kids who need that extra attention. Sincerely, it is already too much to handle, so for someone to assume and guess what you are feeling and thinking or what you want is too much to ask. Make it lighter by just saying it in a respectful way. It is also important to think of how you approach your spouse, your tone of voice and body language determines the success in communication. Always be considerate and speak with a lot of respect rather than make demands and attack.

## Exercise Patience

I am not very good at directions. I thank God for the technology nowadays because we do not necessarily need to check the paper map when travelling. The Satellite Navigation system has become available to many including us. My husband is quite aware of this weakness of mine, so each time we travel and he is driving, he always wants to make sure the GPS is well set before we start the trip. If for any reason the GPS plays up and he asks me to re-enter the address of where we are going, he makes it a point to ask me more than once to check whether I have put in the correct information.

One day we were travelling from London and my husband made a mistake while putting in the information of where we were going. We drove for more than an hour without a sign of where we were going. The trip from London to our place was supposed to take at least fifty minutes. I could see that we were lost because we had missed the correct exit and the GPS could not reroute for some strange reason. I mentioned to him that I think we needed to stop and re-enter the address. He said, the GPS would reroute if at all we were taking the wrong route. We went for another fifteen to twenty minutes, still no sign. Inside I had already figured that we were on a joy ride and not going home. I changed the subject and continued to talk about other things. I decided not to worry and nag him about it.

After one and half hour of driving around London, he realised that we were lost. He then found a place to pull up and check the device. He then realised that he had made a mistake putting in the address. The address he had put was for another area on the other side of London and our home is not even within London.

He corrected the mistake, only then we started to get onto the route home which was another hour from where we were. We laughed about it later and he asked why I did not insist on checking the route earlier.

The moral of this experience is that, it is not always necessary to jump at things and react harshly even though you may know exactly what you are doing.

It is very important for married couples to prioritise being patient to each other. Sometimes people do things unconsciously which can provoke a lot of misunderstanding in the marriage. For example if I had raised my voice to make my husband stop, it was going to spoil our day. Instead I focused on the opportunity to see new things and places and get a joy ride on top.

Be patient when your spouse is talking about something whether important or not so important. When a spouse interrupts the other while talking, they feel as if what they are talking about is being undermined. Even though you sometimes feel the need to interrupt because you have a valid point to put across, patience enables your spouse to be ready when you get to talk as well. We are all guilty at some point when we want to put our point across, we struggle to just sit and listen.

Be patient with your spouse when they exhibit manners which you do not find comfortable or acceptable. Communicate your expectations and need without expecting change overnight. When we expect people to respond a certain way and within a specified time. We create high hopes within ourselves and failure to see immediate change can create friction and abruptness in approach or unnecessary behaviour towards your spouse. We may find ourselves exhibiting reactions that are not particularly pleasant and healthy for the marriage. Take time to work on issues without necessarily putting too much pressure on your spouse to be what you expect.

Remember patience is a virtue. It takes a lot of consideration for a spouse to possess it. Patience helps us understand each other in a more delicate manner. Amidst the confusion and irritation, if we manage to hold it together and treat each other with patience, we can create a happier marriage.

## Chapter 10

# HOW TO ESTABLISH
# GREAT CONNECTION

## How to keep connected to your spouse

Like electricity, we are all aware that for us to have a reaction or a spark from the electricity, the wires have to be well and properly connected. Failure to connect the wires correctly will result in having no electricity to light our houses and to do all things that require electricity.

For a marriage to work, that connection needs to be established. So connection in a marriage is the capability to feel whole with each other in every sense without feeling insecure or uncomfortable. Connections is waking up in the morning with a swollen face looking not so attractive but still feel immense love and want for your spouse. It is hearing your spouse snore the night away but still feel blessed to have them in bed every night. It is knowing each other's weaknesses and making a laugh out of them. It is repeatedly trying to put the puzzle right and failing as many times as you can think of, but still try anyway.

## How to connect with your spouse

### 1. Work and Do Things Together.

I find this point very pertinent in marriage, mostly after a few years in marriage, many spouses tend to ignore the importance of doing things together. Sometimes it is because children take more attention from both parents to the extent that by the end of the day they are so tired to even have a meaningful talk together. It can also be the mere passiveness, just the lack of drive to actually incorporate each other in some of the activities that we can do together and have fun while doing it.

It is important to take time to even do the dishes together, dress the children together, go for a walk together, do charity work together. All these acts are a nourishment of the bond between married couples.

Go out for dinner together once in a while. Look for interesting events you can attend together. You can always have something to talk about when you do things together.

## 2. Physical Touch

Touch is a way of communicating love to each other. It pronounces each other's presence and want. Touching does not only happen in the bedroom when you are making love with your spouse. It can happen anywhere and it drives the need to be intimate with each other. Holding hands while taking a walk, patting each other here and there, leaning on each other are all gestures of love that make spouses feel special and that, you are mine and I am not ashamed to show it to the world.

Personally I am a touchy feely person, I enjoy leaning on my husband, sometimes we go out where we have to sit for a long time. I cannot feel back pain for sitting upright when God gave me a husband to hold on to and to lean on. I thank God each day for that blessing.

## 3. Be romantic

Again being romantic is not just the act of having sex. It is all that happens leading to it. Connecting with your spouse has one unique characteristic that is not found in any other relationship and that is, **'romance'**. We all love our parents, siblings, friends but these are people we cannot be romantically involved with.

My best friend lives in another continent and we meet once in a while. When we do organise to meet, we enjoy booking a hotel, go for a spa, safari and other activities to bond, catch up and inspire each other. One thing with this great friendship is, we can never be romantically involved. We have a different relationship. The only person who I can therefore share intimacy and romance with, is Courage, my husband.

Take time to invest in the quality time you have intimately. Create an ambient, light candles, dress provocative, talk sweetly and tenderly, be feisty. Adam and Eve were naked and not ashamed, your bodies belong together, take time to explore each other without shame.

## 4. Eye contact

Eyes are a human being's reception, the eyes can communicate without necessarily talking. When people go on interviews, one of the things the interviewer looks at is your eye contact. It spells confidence, enthusiasm and drive. Looking into your partner's eyes when you are talking or listening to them communicates, 'I am giving all my heart and attention to you. I'm not distracted by anything else. You are my priority'.

Turning off all distractions and focusing solely on your partner means you are choosing to make a connection.

## 5. Show interest in your spouse's interests

As I have highlighted in the previous chapters that spouses will never have same likes and interests all the time. My husband loves football, and I honestly do not see the fun in it. I do not watch TV that much but I like reality TV shows and he honestly does not see anything that fun in my favourite programmes. However I noticed that when I am not at home when my programme is running or he notices a programme similar to what I like, he records it for me to watch later. I do not take that for granted, I take it he cares for my pass time too even though he cannot sit and watch with me the whole time.

With football I struggle to sit there for ninety minutes seeing him jump at every goal opportunity. However I do escort him to the Sunday leisure football game that he participates in with fellow church members. You do not necessarily need to adopt likes and interests that are not yours but the support you show one way or the other can make all the difference.

## 6. Share Humour

From the list of expectations that most single people have when they are looking for the right person to marry or to get married to. A good sense of humour is mainly in the top five of the preferences. Everybody needs and wants a lighter moment in life, too much seriousness and no laughter in the marriage can be toxic. Create moments of jokes at every opportunity that you get and be free to express your crazy thoughts to your spouse. Laughter is one good way of relieving stress, when we laugh, the body releases the endorphins that causes stress. It is a remedy for physical health as well as any kind of relationship including marriage.

Talk about your past experiences, the blunders you have made in life, embarrassing moments and other things that can create an environment of laughter.

## 7. Simple gestures of love

My husband always helps out in the house when he can. One day he said to me, 'I want you to have one full day you can just rest, relax and do nothing'. So he said, ' every Sunday you can sleep all you want, I will do everything in the house including making breakfast for you in bed'. I felt so esteemed just from hearing him being considerate to me like that. Every Sunday besides Sabbath, has become the best day of the week.

As I have said before, the best things in life are for free. You do not need to have money to show love and care for your spouse. All you need is the will to make your other happy and many ideas will always come your way. Treat your spouse to a massage, help him/her to dress up, comb their hair, run a bath. These are things you do not need to do on a daily basis, if you manage a small gesture of love once a week, it strengthens the bond and connection.

When my husband and I were on our annual family trip in Morocco. We went to climb the Atlas Mountains and as we were climbing, my husband would hold my hand and help me climb the mountain, he would pause to ask me if I was tired and needed some rest. He made me feel like a baby for a minute, who does not want that.

I also enjoy writing random sweet messages and complimenting him as many times as possible, it makes me feel good just doing it. I did not take any massage lessons but I also enjoy giving my husband massages. In the end we have set aside at least one day a week when we can put our daughter to bed and give each other full body massages.

All the things I have listed, do not need a penny to do but they make all the difference in a marriage, they make all the challenges we face insignificant.

## Chapter 11

# REACHING MARITAL MATURITY

I have called this topic reaching marital maturity because it is the stage where couples feel they are in it for the long ride and their union is worth every penny. Give for example a fruit, when a fruit is said to have reached maturity and ready to be consumed, it means the fruit has stood the test of harsh climates and threats from different kinds of insects and worms.

I know many of us look at a fruit and never think of the challenges that fruit could have faced inorder to reach the point of being desirable to eat. We somehow feel well it is just a fruit and in season ready to be eaten.

It is the same in marriage, for a marriage to be called mature, it ought to have gone through turbulent times and the people in it are able to look at the challenge and find peace with it. Spouses are bound to annoy each other quite a lot there is no two ways about it. I was listening to one preacher on TV who said, if you have not argued with your spouse then you are not married yet. If you have not faced challenges in your life then you have not started to live.

It is clear that our perception of life and marriage may be to see everything in life sailing as smoothly as we envisage it to be. The presence of challenges in our life can make us think life is treating us so wrong and all of a sudden you start to look around you and see all the smiling happy faces. In your mind it appears as if oh everyone else is happy except me and you start to beat yourself about it. The truth of the matter is being happy does not mean the absence of problems. It does not mean other people's lives are going according to how they want it to be. It only means some people decide to focus on the positive side of life rather than the problems that they face because problems are part and parcel of life to and are meant to refine us.

In marriage when you reach to a point where your spouse does something that really makes you want to raise that voice and tell them your piece of mind or threaten to leave your home. When you reach a point in your marriage where your spouse says something hurtful, belittles you, continues with that same weakness, you tell them one thing and they do the other, they seem not to be bothered about anything in your love life. When your spouse does all this to you but you decide to be calm and deal with it with lots of love, consideration and without remorse. When you get to a point where nothing wrong they do annoys you then I personally call that marital maturity. It shows that the marriage has stood the test of time to the extent that nomatter how the devil wants to resurface, he is already defeated in that marriage.

In retrospect most couples who reach marital maturity actually feel that they have wasted so much time and energy on things that were not so important. Things that were not healthy or beneficial to the marriage, however it is important to go through challenges and device a better way to deal with them inorder to maintain harmony and peace in the home.

As much as reaching marital maturity is definitely difficult. Getting to a point where you laugh about your spouse's weakness and not get all worked up about it is achievable if your main goal in your marriage is to be happy and to maintain peace.

## Understanding the Marital Stages

## Stage 1 : 1-3 years

This is the heat stage just after marriage. Spouses are just in the world of love and discovering each other's strengths and weaknesses, annoyances and excitements.

This stage can carry a lot of mixed emotions which can include confusion and shock. Most people call this stage the honeymoon stage where the couple is more intimate without kids around. Practically this is the most difficult stage in a marriage. Eventhough a couple may be all excited about each other. This is also a stage where spouses discover each other's bad habits and behaviour which can possibly annoy and destroy the love between a married couple.

This is a stage where it can be difficult to apply the, leave and cleave biblical principle. Some spouses may be so attached to their families to the extent that they want to carry their families with them into the marriage. This can be toxic to the newlyweds. This is the stage where you come to terms with the fact that you are no longer independent. Everything you do, your spouse has to know, you share everything including time and friends. Literally this is when you realise that your freedom is kind of gone because you owe somebody an explanation for all your actions.

Most divorces also happen at this stage, sometimes people cannot take the surprises that come with marriage and the best way for them is to quit rather than cope with the situation. When people get married, they have this picture perfect vision of how marriage is going to be. They imagine and envision making a lot of love, laughing together no intruders or unannounced visitors, no unfaithfulness, no communicating with people of the opposite sex, no financial problems.

The minute you enter into it you begin to face a lot of unanticipated disturbances and annoyances.

You may experience that, each time you plan to spend the weekend with your spouse, you receive your spouse's family members who have come to stay indefinitely in your tiny flat. The visitors may just come without prior communication about it. This can make you feel disappointed and irritated with your spouse and her/his family for not consulting you. The family may also put financial burden on you, you find out that they have taken luxury stuff on credit for you to pay.

You may face challenges of transparency. Your spouse may have questionable behaviour and they may keep a lot of secrets with them.

You may realise that your spouse is not all that he portrayed to be before you got married. You may start to face insults over silly issues or even physical abuse. You hear that they have children out of wedlock yet you were never told about it.

All these issues can easily break you. As sad as it may seem when newly married couples divorce or separate just after getting married. The challenges are real and not everyone is going to manage to cope in some situations. You need to applaud yourself if you have successfully passed this stage.

## <u>Tips for the Newlyweds</u>

1. Learn to compromise. The way you used to do things as a single person may not work as a married person. Identify things you can adjust inorder to accommodate each other. If you used to eat cold food and take away everyday before marriage, you might need to take cookery lessons and cook hearty warm meals with your spouse.

2. Do not expect too much. High expectations always kill the momentum in the marriage. Adapt to what is there and create room for improvement from both of you. Appreciate what each brings to the table and communicate where you need to do more work.

3. Embrace change. It may be intimidating to wake up to someone who has to have your diary and somehow know what you are doing and where you are going all the time. Your spouse may be good at playing the guitar and he/she just pulls it out even when you really want a relaxing time without noise. Embracing this new person in your life means you accept them as they are and they can be themselves around you.

4. Work together especially financially. It improves your bond and unity.

5. Adorn yourself for your spouse. Looking presentable and smelling nice around your spouse keeps his/her eyes glued to you. Be pleasant to be with, invest time to make yourself look good and be a joy to look at.

6. Invest in quality time. This is a must, be playful and do not be too serious all the time.

7. Learn to talk with calmness. There is nothing as annoying as living with a quarrelsome person. You do not always need to raise your voice inorder to be heard. When you talk with calmness, you reap better rewards.

8. Choose your battles wisely. Not all battles are worth fighting. Identify battles that can bring a negative impact on the marriage if not discussed for example infidelity, communication, in laws, finances. These are just a few of the pertinent issues you can have a sit down for. However little things like leaving the toothpaste tube open, socks put in the wrong drawer, are not necessarily issues you should get so worked up on. Focus on important issues.

9. Be transparent. Do not engage in private activities. When you get married, you become indebted to your spouse with regards to your day to day life and activities.

**10.** Forge a cordial relationship with your in laws. Even though they do not really like you or you do not like them. It is important that you maintain a working relationship where you can still visit and talk without necessarily becoming close.

**11.** More romance. This is extremely important, you both married for nothing else but intimacy. Children are the fruit of the intimacy you share as married couples. Invest a lot of time in making this activity special.

**12.** Be patient. Allow growth in your marriage. Change does not happen overnight, it takes time. Embrace your spouse and their weaknesses and give time and space for improvement.

## Stage 2:

### 3-5 years – Just Take It

After all the storm and tempest of emotions and exhaustion, there comes the time to reflect and pave a way forward. As I mentioned in stage one, you have to applaud yourself if you have passed the critical first three years, the most difficult for almost **eighty percent** of marriages.

Around stage two you would have learnt all about your spouse's weaknesses and strengths. Weaknesses which you cannot change. This is when you allow yourself to swallow character and behaviour that annoys you from your spouse. In other words you learn to live with their negatives without you getting so worked up about it.

With time you actually learn that living and sharing your life with someone is not as easy but you can make a comfortable situation out of it. This is the most important part in marriage as you learn to let go most of the issues which used to cause a lot of differences in your marriage. Many couples actually feel and regret having wasted precious time worrying and dwelling on the negatives, trying to win battles and to have the last word which in the end only causes unhappiness unnecessarily.

One of the couples I spoke to actually said, we have realised that the devil and the enemy in our marriage is ourselves and upon realising how good life can be if you take a positive approach. Now they spend most of their time trying to maximise on spending more quality time together including the time lost in the past years.

## Stage 3: 5 years +

## Maturity

As we all know maturity comes with age, and as more years pass in marriage, the marriage becomes mature. The people involved in it become mature in the way they approach issues and their relationship in general. It is rare to still see a couple who have been together for over ten years still having emotionally heated arguments. I am not ruling out the possibility but the rate decreases as years go by.

When I say marital maturity, this is where two people feel a complete sense of belonging. This is where you can stay with your hair unkempt for two days and your spouse cannot be bothered and sometimes they can't even notice. This is when you make fun out of each other's weaknesses and talk to each other more like friends. This is the stage you are care free, you say what you want and feel without fear of being judged or it being used against you.

It all sounds rosy but in practice the problems may still be present but the way they are approached is different to the way you do for example in the first year of marriage. Most of mature marriage divorces are mainly caused by infidelity and lack of connection in the marriage, but overall couples are stronger and mellow in their approach to marriage.

Maturity in marriage is an important stage which we should all embrace and applaud ourselves as a big achievement. With nearly fifty percent of all marriages worldwide ending in divorce. Which means almost one in every two marriages will end in divorce, it is refreshing to still see couples standing the test of time and passing the difficult stages.

I was watching an interview on marriage enrichment testimony series. A couple who have been married for more than twenty years. They looked very happy and in love with each other. As I was watching and listening to them relating their marital journey, it came clear to me that they had gone through the highest and the lowest. When you listen to a powerful couple saying, the only solution we had at the time was divorce or separation. It makes you realise how the marriage institution has been and will always pose extreme challenges nomatter how you might want to overlook it sometimes.

What captivated me the most is how this couple managed to change the weaknesses they had which caused the other to feel inadequate and unloved. This couple learnt good lessons through other couples they had to help with marital issues. They were given the power to help other couples to solve their problems at the same time they were literally in need of marital intervention themselves. As I have mentioned in the previous chapters, as married couples, we do learn a lot from each other and from other couples. Sometimes we learn from the bad things happening in other peoples marriages then we realise how bad that would be if it was happening in your marriage. We also learn from couples with relatively good relationships, it encourages us to work on our differences.

Like any other relationship, maturity highlights that you have survived the bitterness, sleepless nights, crying your eyeballs out, you might actually have packed your bags to leave a few times. Going through all that but still managing to soldier on and remaining happy together, that explains maturity.

The reason why most people believe in companies which have been running for a longer time is the maturity that they would have acquired overtime. Big and established companies have a better way of dealing with the problems faced by clients because of the experience that they possess therefore even smaller and newer companies tend to seek advice from the long running companies because of the maturity.

# Chapter 12

# PRINCIPLES OF MARRIAGE

## Maintaining your principles even in the face of adversity

To start with, I would like to explain the term, 'principle' in the marriage sense. Principle means believing and executing what is right and acceptable in your marriage. When I was growing up, one of the main principles instilled in me by my parents was to be kind to others even if people are hostile to me. Yes, in many cases and situations I was tempted to be rude and unkind but my principles kept me in line and I realised that with principles came integrity and respect.

In the marriage, spouses get tempted in many different ways due to the many external pressures and misunderstandings in the home. One of the most common temptations that lure people into giving up their principles is lack of intimacy from one or both parties for one reason or the other. The lack of communication as to how certain issues can be solved can trigger losing your principles. However after all this is said and done, most successful marriages survive on principles coupled with other factors that make the marriage work.

## How to maintain your principles as a spouse

> Remind yourself, know and understand the value of respecting your spouse and the reason why you are together in the first place.

> Communicate your grievances as much as you can. If you cannot solve the problem, seek advice from professionals or a trusted person. Sometimes people use assumption a lot in marriage which in most cases turns out to be biased therefore seek to free your mind and heart by talking about your problem to your partner.

> Surround yourselves with positive people. By en large our lives are partly shaped by the people we choose to associate with. If we constantly associate with people who are negative about marriage because theirs did not succeed, then the likelihood of wavering from our principles is

high. It is also refreshing to associate with people and other couples who cherish and love each other even though they may have problems. This in turn can encourage and reinforce our marital principles.

> Never go with the wind, think before you act. There was a young couple whose marriage was on the rocks due to infidelity and family involvement. One of the problems that the husband had was he could take anything at face value without being rational and objective about it. So each time his friends would come to his home and take him out to drink and have fun, in most cases he would return home after midnight when the wife has already tired from waiting. The next day when the wife asked why he came late, he would always blame his friends for influencing him.

He also had a family who enjoyed telling him what to do in his marriage even disregarding the fact that he had a wife who deserved respect and honour. Most of the time that his siblings or parents asked him for something or to do something, he would just do without consulting the spouse. Whether it was a good and viable decision for him it did not matter, he simply followed whatever anyone told him to do.

This without a doubt caused a big rift in his marriage to the extent of threatening divorce because the wife did not feel safe with a husband who did not have any principles to follow.

Principles help us to mould not just our marriages and relationships, but also our lives improve in quality. I have heard many therapists say it is important to be happy and principled within, once you are happy and principled within yourself then it is much easier to be principled even when you are married with a family.

> Pray for your marriage, they say, 'A family that prays together, stays together'. In James 5:16, Confess your faults to one another, and pray for one another, that ye may be healed. When we make prayer our business and focus in our marriage, it gives us the energy and power to accept differences, it guides us to forgive one another. Spouses who pray together create more bond and connection overtime.

## Nine benefits of being prayerful in marriage

1. Prayer makes you humble in life, with God and to your spouse and family.

2. Prayer gives you conscience and the capability to be considerate to your spouse.

3. Prayer makes everything alright, it makes you heal from deeper wounds within.

4. Prayer encourages unity in the marriage.

5. Prayer makes spouses look at each other as a blessing and it makes spouses appreciate each other for everything.

6. Prayer makes people change from bad to good.

7. Prayer covers all the wrong doings

8. Prayer Instils hope

9. Prayer embraces all situations, loves and forgives always

When we continue to pray together and to pray for each other, God can reveal himself through our spouses by the way they treat us and maintain the home. God gives wisdom in marriage, even today you see a lot of well educated people getting divorced more and more. It shows us that marriage is only run by God's wisdom and not by how well learned or how much we have achieved. Therefore the more we spend time with God as a couple, the more we feel his presence in our lives.

## Resist Temptation

I attended one of the late Nancy Van Pelt's marriage seminars in the UK in 2011. One of the things she mentioned was, the eye that wanders. She highlighted that men in particular should teach themselves to turn their necks the other way when they see what looks interesting and palatable. I personally think, women should adopt the same principle because more and more women have become more exposed to infidelity. Good morals and values have generally declined significantly over the past few decades to both men and women.

Inorder to succeed in whatever we do, we do have to show that we can stand the test of time, have the capability to deal with the challenges and temptations that we face. I give for example, bank tellers, they have thousands and thousands of money that pass through their hands on a daily basis. Money which they do not have control over or the right to use. Yet their salaries are a fraction of what they handle within a day or just a few hours. Sometimes they handle money even when they do not have money to buy food on the table or send children to school. However they continue to be faithful to their employer because failure to do so can result in worse situations like going to prison if you succumb to the temptation.

The impact of succumbing to temptation is more cruel than resisting the temptation. Men and women in the workforce meet many different people of the opposite sex on a daily basis. Some who appear to look more dazzling and well structured than their spouses. Women can meet men who seem to have more courtesy by pulling the chair or open the door for them. Men who seem to talk to them in a soft, caring and passionate voice. That may seem more romantic and out of this world, but in my culture there is a saying that goes, 'The Bee, stay in one place, flowers of the world never end'. In my Shona language it's, '**Zingizi gonyera pamwe maruva enyika haaperi'.**

We cannot avoid temptation coming our way, but we can fight it and be victorious in our marital goals. Temptation has caused over thirty percent of the divorce rate in the world.

In James 1 vs. 13-17, when tempted, no one should say, 'God is tempting me. For God cannot be tempted by evil nor does he tempt anyone, but each one is tempted when, by his own evil desire, he is dragged away and enticed. The after desire has conceived, it gives both to sin, and sin when it is full grown, gives birth to death. Do not be deceived my dear brothers. Every good and perfect gift is from above, coming down from the father of the heavenly lights, who does not change like shifting shadows.

# Chapter 13

# DEALING WITH PETTY
# AND REAL ANGER

When I got married, I was so happy to have a husband and to be called MRS. My husband made me feel special in every way he could. One of the problems I had was whenever we had a disagreement about something silly. I would spend the whole day if not two very angry and I would give him silent treatment. This was a little habit that was taking a big chunk of my marital happiness. Each time I was angry, my husband would continue to be happy and each time he would show that he is not bothered by my anger, I would feel more and more anger even feeling pity for myself because he appeared to not notice that I was angry. I wanted him to look so worried about me because I was angry.

Six months into the marriage, we had a marital assessment and looked into what it is that we could improve on to make our marriage better and more enjoyable. One of the things that me and my husband highlighted was the importance of making use of each moment that God has given us to be happy and celebrate each other. My husband mentioned how getting angry with each other for the whole day or two was not very healthy for our marriage. Of course, I felt bad when I was angry over a small difference but sometimes we do not realise that we constantly feed our little bad habits that can eventually cost us in the end.

We then adopted a motto in our marriage that, 'Let us cherish each other, we might not see each other again tomorrow'. After that assessment, nomatter how we find differences in thoughts or interests, we do not allow that to take our happiness away. The bible says in Ephesians 4:26. 'Be angry and do not sin, let not the sun go down upon your wrath. As married couples we are bound to be angry at each other but again the bottom line is, how we choose to deal with, 'IT' that matters.

I realised that, I do not want to lose more hours or days of my life getting angry and miserable over things that can be dealt with amicably. That feeling was kind of a turning point for me. I realised that if I want to enjoy my life let alone my marriage, I had to change sooner than later. All the anger was not just affecting my husband, it was affecting me inside and out. I vowed to myself from then on never to spend a day angry no matter who angers me. I made the decision to be happy and prioritise the most important things in my life. Believe me after realising my flaw and rectifying it, I became the happiest person in the world, my outlook in life changed.

I thank God for actually making me realise my problem and have the will to make a turn for the right. Psychologically, anger, if prolonged can be detrimental to health and can cause immense stress and pressure to the human wellbeing. Like stress, when angry, the body produces adrenaline and cortisol, which are the hormones that causes stress.

There are many situations, circumstances that we face in marriage. Situations that do nothing but cause us grief and hurt, situations that threaten our sanity. Many marriages face problems with unfaithfulness, domestic differences, angry spouses, troublesome in laws, failure to conceive, abusive spouses and the list is endless. All these challenges are the devil's work threatening to destroy the marriage institution and they can trigger anger in a spouse. This anger can be shown in different ways, sometimes silent treatment, revenge, withdrawal from being intimate with spouse, rough and excruciating words to spouse, physical violence and more.

As sad as it seems, that is the reality we live in today. Anger robs families of happiness and peace. Many people have died due to medical conditions triggered by anger like stress, depression, high or low blood pressure, harbouring anger is like nurturing your own death. Anger has made small problems which could be solved to escalate to unimaginable heights including divorce, suicide and even killing each other. When I was working in Namibia, within the four year period I lived there, I heard more than a hundred cases of partners who killed each other over a small argument. That is how bad anger can get.

## Steps to dealing with anger in a marriage

> Compose and calm yourself, as difficult as it might sound especially at the peak of an argument. It is in the mind, yes you can control your anger and your spouse's anger by maintaining calmness and staying composed. Learn to focus on how to solve the problem instead of fighting to win the argument or to prove your spouse wrong. Have you ever asked yourself, if you win the argument, what benefit does it give to your family? It is not always about winning. It is about finding common ground and meeting each other half way to make your life happy and worthwhile.

> Think of the long term consequences, if you take time to think of the impact that anger can have on your marriage and children. You might

realise how much time and quality time you waste by using anger as a tool to express your concerns in the marriage.

➢ Pray and Talk to someone about it. For Christians prayer can do wonders. It can take that whole weight off your shoulders. Believe and leave it to God, he knows what is best for you. Sometimes we feel the weight is too much, it helps if you talk to God or a prayer partner, trusted friend or family, never keep toxic feelings in side, they breed more anger and hurt which may result in life threatening medical conditions.

➢ Restrategize, when you feel you have a problem managing your anger. Find new ways that you can use to deal with anger rather than confrontation and toxic behaviour. For example, you can decide that each time you feel anger inside you, take leave for a few minutes to think and to calm down. You can decide to go for a jog or walk, you can visit a good friend or meet for a cup of tea. There are many ways you can adopt to deal with anger. Remember you can make or destroy your life, the choice to be happy and to have peace is in your hands.

➢ Spouses must avoid talking too much or become too defensive when you see that your spouse is very angry. Give them time to calm down. Trying to explain things when somebody is very angry can only make matters worse therefore avoid that by talking about it when you are both calm. Talking over each other when angry makes it difficult for your point to be heard, instead it can breed more problems that could be avoided such as saying derogatory words to spouse.

# Chapter 14

# EMBRACING OUR DIFFERENCES

People are born different and have been exposed to a lot of different situations. I boarded a bus from Zimbabwe to South Africa with a young lady who was going to see her husband in South Africa after a long period apart from each other. She seemed so excited and looking forward to spending quality time with her husband.

Within the conversation I had with her, she constantly mentioned how her husband behaved so childish at times. She was blaming it on him being the last born in his family who got anything he wanted and would get away with any mischief. She mentioned how he sometimes spend most of his salary on very expensive clothes without putting any savings aside. She mentioned how he would get angry over silly things and more. The most interesting thing she said at the end is, she had learnt to accept him as he is and was looking for better ways to deal with his weaknesses.

God created us different, sometimes there are habits or weaknesses that your spouse may have that pushes you to the wall and you may be tempted to retaliate in a way that can possibly worsen the situation. Sometimes you find that your spouse has a lot of anger inside that he even embarrasses you when you are in public if you misunderstand each other on something. Sometimes it may be just the lack of general emotional support or even lack of sweet words.

Some people grew up in very difficult situations or went through difficulties at some stage in their life. You may expect to get kisses everyday, words of praise, support in what you do but what you get may be totally the opposite. This does not mean your spouse is heartless, yes it might be that in some cases but some people do not know how to show love because they never experienced it growing up or in their lives. They may actually be thinking they are doing a lot without knowing you are expecting more from them.

It takes time for a spouse to understand if things are not going the way that they imagined or expected. I wrote about the stages of marriage, the knowledge of these stages can help spouses to grow and nurture each other even with their weaknesses. When you get to the point of maturity in marriage then that means you become numb to your spouse's weaknesses and see them as part of life.

The most important thing however is to also take note of your weaknesses. I do understand that it is easier to look at how the other person is treating you rather than how you are treating them. I think the more we look at ourselves and our flaws within a marriage, the more we seek to find a solution that can make both our weaknesses adaptable or rather easier to deal with.

There is also a threshold on how that weakness is exhibited, if it involves adultery or physical abuse, then we cannot classify that as a mere weakness but a problem that needs immediate intervention.

Embracing each other's differences means a lot in a marriage, we can classify that as unconditional love. We often take this word and our vows for granted. I have heard many people saying, I did not know it was going to be like this and in my mind I am thinking, what is the meaning of, 'for better for worse' then. This is a question that each couple has to ask themselves.

The more you embrace each other as you are, the happier you can be in your marriage.

# Chapter 15

# INTIMACY

When people talk about intimacy, we rush to think it is mostly the sexual act. However as much as sex is one of the key aspects of intimacy there are different ways of being intimate in the marriage. First of all let us define intimacy, from a psychological perspective. Intimacy refers to closeness, togetherness, bonding, rapport, a moment of calmness, heart sharing and understanding. The definition is broad and can be taken from different angles but closeness surpasses them all.

For any existing marriage to succeed, for it to stand the test of time and the pressures that come with it, there should be intimacy. If you are in a marriage and there is no intimacy then we can classify that as a business partnership for running a home and children but not a marriage. As harsh as it may sound, the reality is if our marriages do not experience some kind of intimacy one way or the other then what difference is it from all other relationships you have with friends, colleagues and family?

## Types of Marital Intimacy

### Sex

One of the most unique gift in marriage is the intimacy that spouses share sexually. It is one of the things that one cannot get from a friend, parent or siblings. God created every human being in a way that at a certain stage in life, their bodies yearn for affection and intimacy. In 1 Corinthians 7:2-4 The husband should fulfil his marital duty to his wife, and likewise the wife to her husband. The wife's body does not belong to her alone but also to her husband. In the same way, the husband's body does not belong to him alone but also to his wife. Do not deprive each other except by mutual consent and for a time, so that you may devote yourselves to prayer.

I think the majority of people get married because they want to experience the gift of sex together. I have not heard anyone saying they are marrying so that they can build a house together or so that they can go on holidays and take care of parents together. As much as there are supporting components when people get married, sex is the main reason why people get married. That is why the bible clearly states that both spouses should fulfil each other's sexual desire unless there is a valid reason not to.

Sex is important in a marriage, it does not only fulfil the sexual desire in the human being but it also brings the gift of children. The flowers that give us joy, pride, happiness and that we cherish every day. Sex makes people happy, it also contributes to how well we do in life, be it at work or any kind of commitments we have. Medically like laughter it helps release endorphins that causes stress. So if you have had a hard stressful day at work, try to have sex with your spouse, it improves the mood and a positive outlook to life.

Sex brings spouses closer, it strengthens the bond of marriage because you are one flesh it even makes better sense.

I would say sex is the most intimate way, it is the highest point in the marriage union. On that note, let us not forget the importance of faithfulness. Many problems that we face today, problems of HIV/AIDS, extra-marital affairs and illegitimate children are also caused by sex which means as much as it is a good thing, God blesses sexual intimacy shared by married couples, anything else can only bring misery and grief to the whole society.

## Sex from the men's Perspective

Men and women were created differently, physically and mentally. The way that men and women look at things and think is quite different. That is why you see women more interested in doing shopping and going to the toilet as a group than men. The things that men enjoy are not always the things that make women excited for example football, there is a very low percentage of women who enjoy football in general and yet almost eighty percent of men enjoy and love football.

With regard to sex, men and women have a different outlook and expectations too. Men spend most of their time in the day thinking about sex. I interviewed three different men on this aspect and all of them expressed that besides work and football, the only other thing they are quite passionate about is sex. Men do marry mainly for sex, they do not marry just because they want to have children or they wish to build a life and develop with a companion. The children and family development come as a bonus if I can say. A male friend of mine related that, if at all a disaster happens to the family, men think of their wives first and women think of their children first. Get me right, this does not mean men do not care about building a family besides sex but they are more sex centred than women.

Men look at sex as a fulfilment, it is something that they always want to achieve in life. If we look at the stories of adultery that are reported on a daily basis. People do not focus much on the men because the society considers the men as a macho if he manages to lure many women sexually.

Men always think they are good in bed and they yearn for that appreciation from their spouse. Sometimes for variety of reasons like pre-mature ejaculation or erectile dysfunction which is quite normal to some men especially over the age of 50. Women may lose interest and disengage from being sexually intimate with their spouses.

The feeling of **'rejection'** can potentially drive men into having extra-marital affairs for the sake of fulfilling that need, that id. According to Sigmund Freud, we are all born with id. It is based on a human being's pleasure principle, in other words it is the want of what feels good at the time with no consideration for the reality of the situation.

Men want women to be more adventurous in bed by trying new things that enhance their fantasy. For example, a lot of men prefer sex with the light on because what attracts them is the woman's body and the woman's expression.

Most times when a man looks at his woman, he is looking for a sex appeal, something that triggers the intimate desire. He is looking at the way a woman walks, talks and conduct herself around him. The more gracious and groomed the woman is, the more the desire a man gets to be intimate.

The quality of sex that a man experiences with his wife determines the frequency of intimacy present in the marriage. Men are not quite fond of the headaches that normally surface during night time. It is quite a put off for men to think intimately about their spouse the whole day and then they come home, somebody has a terrible headache. They take this as an indirect way of rejection.

From the three interviews I conducted, in marriage, men prefer their women dressed less or not dressed at all during the night. They want to feel and connect to the body physically. Winter time may be knocking at the door and you are so tempted to pull that onesie for bed. As I mentioned earlier, Adam and Eve were naked and not ashamed. Being naked with each other in marriage is not a sin.

## Sex from the women's Perspective

Women possess a very sensitive and quite dynamic nature in them. They do not just marry for the sake of sexual pleasure. Women can get married because of age, security and to have children.

With regard to sex in the marriage, women tend to be more on the emotional side. They want to feel loved, cuddled, kissed and valued. Women want to feel a love connection with the spouse. If a woman has not been treated well throughout the day, then the likelihood of her engaging intimately is quite low. Women are not always ready for sex which means the response is cylical, it means women experience times when they want sex and times when they do not feel they want sex.

It takes a lot to get a woman to engage in sex especially when they are not in the right mood. A lot of cranking is required for a woman to respond. Due to the fear of their husbands cheating, many women pretend or rather fake to be enjoying sex even though they may not be feeling anything.

However women can warm up to sex if they are treated romantically throughout the day, women want to hear the sweet words. They desire more foreplay. Women also feel good when their spouse compliments them on their looks, their body and many other sweet things a man can say to a woman. More work is required for a woman to feel sexually satisfied.

The hormonal fluctuation that women go through due to their menses is one of the reasons why women are cylical (sometimes) and men are acylical (always ready). Also women tend to get distracted easily during sex, any thought or disturbance can take a woman from nine to zero. Therefore for a marriage to be more enjoyable, it is important to understand how different each spouse is from the other. It reduces the risk of having high expectations and opens up the need to communicate preferences and way forward.

## Praying together

I was reading Nancy Van Pelt's Highly Effective Marriage and she says one of the noble things that married couples can do is to pray together for each other. Besides the normal family prayers, spouses have to pray for their relationship including their sex life.

The fact that when we talk to God, we are trying to be intimate with the highest power. It only makes sense that as couples you should spend some intimate time together with the Lord.

Prayer brings families together, as they say, a family that prays together stays together. It makes perfect sense because God rejoices in married couples who take time to talk to him together.

## Words of Praise

One of the trends I have noticed on the people's wedding invitation cards since I was little was the extracts from King Solomon's book in the bible. Something peculiar seemed to captivate people in the book of Solomon. The beautiful, profound, poetic words, words that can calm the heart and soul, words that make a spouse leap with joy and happiness.

Proverbs 31:10, a wife of noble character who can find? She is worth far more than rubies.

People want to feel special, and when you are married you do not need to buy anything for your spouse for them to feel special. God gave us the gift of words, unlimited, the choice is yours. Telling your spouse how precious they are to you means the world to them. Personally I love words, I love to hear beautiful sweet words from my husband, it makes me feel good and special. I also enjoy telling my husband the sweetest words I can think of, it makes me feel good to do that and most of the time when I tell him sweet words, he is lost for words. Before I got married, I always envisioned a husband who wakes me up to poetic verses and kisses. Beautiful words can bring you even more closer than physical intimacy that is how important it is to whisper those sweet words to your significant other even if you are experiencing problems.

# Chapter 16

# MONEY MATTERS

## When Money Takes Over

Yes, the world revolves around money and economic stability. The focus of life is based on finances, people wake up everyday looking for money and sleep thinking about it. This is a fact and a reality that there is not much we can do or change about it.

Within a marriage, it so happens that money also takes centre stage in the smooth running of the home as well as the relationship. As the bible clearly states that, 'the love of money is the root of all evil'. There are many marriages that have broken and are still breaking as a result of inharmonious money issues.

Below is a true story of a migrant family in the United Kingdom:

## Financial Transition

When I met this family for an interview, they had just gone through a divorce and three years later, realised they belonged together, it was only money that separated them.

## Real Life Story (pseudo names used)

Lisa and Jake had left home from Africa to the United Kingdom to seek greener pastures during the economic instability that swept their beautiful country.

Jake was working as a top marketing manager at a very big parastatal. He was a good provider in the home and would even manage to take care of the extended family and send his siblings to good schools. Lisa by that time was a nursing student at the capital hospital.

When the two met, they fell in love and Lisa fell pregnant just before she finished her Nursing Diploma. She had the child and went back to finish school with the support from Jake. They then decided to formalise their relationship and they had a wedding and became a family.

Life seemed perfect and ever happy, they even had their second child. In 2001, Jake's company suffered retrenchment and unfortunately, he became one of the casualties. This affected them financially to the extent that they had to downsize their living standards. Although Lisa was working, her salary alone could not sustain the lifestyle that they had with Jake working with the company. He eventually found another similar job four months later. This was a much needed rescue from their financial downfall. Whilst they were celebrating now in 2002, the money market took a turn for the worst with inflation skyrocketing and affecting the price of commodities.

Prices could hike anytime within minutes or seconds. During that time they say, every time you wanted to buy something, it was better to buy it then instead of going to another shop to compare prices because by the time you decide in which shop to buy, the prize would have gone up by fifty or a hundred percent or even more. Salaries remained the same but commodities were hiking prices and interest rates were unbelievable.

The situation led to them trying the Diaspora for greener pastures. During that time the UK was employing a lot of nurses from other countries, many nurses had already left and were sustaining families back home. They decided that Lisa was going to try and find a job in the UK. She was the one who settled in the UK first and then the family followed later.

## Reversal of Roles

When Jake arrived in the UK, he stayed for a few months at home taking care of the children while Lisa went to work. He would take the children to and from school every day. He would also do the house chores and sometimes Lisa would get so frustrated getting home to find the house dirty. She was working very long hours that it would be hard for her to get home and start cleaning and cooking, she could only do so when she had off days.

Life went on like that for a while but inside. Jake felt like his ego was knocked down as he was doing what he always thought was the women's or the nanny's job. This led to him being aggressive at times because he had come from being a well respected manager who had people make tea for him at the office to him being the nanny and housekeeper.

On the other hand Lisa felt as if she had all the power in the house because she was bringing in the money and had also brought the husband to the first world country. She would refuse to send some money to his family back home and she was no longer comfortable discussing family finances with her husband. She would tell him that there are many bills to pay, she cannot support his family.

Jake then looked for a job and got one in a warehouse where they would pack frozen products in cold rooms and picking very heavy stuff. Jake was not accustomed, so he left and found another job as a carer in a care home. He was still not satisfied but he felt it was better than nothing. His salary was not anywhere close to what Lisa earned. They started arguing over who was going to pay for what each month, it became a battle just planning their day to day expenses.

Lisa decided to build a house in Africa without the husband's knowledge and all the documents were in her name. When Jake discovered this, he was very angry and became physically abusive to her. They kissed goodbye to the happiness and peace that they once had. Lisa packed her bags and moved out of the house and filed for divorce two months later.

Now they later realised that they were meant to be together, they are living together after they received therapy. The best part is that they have put all properties they acquired in both their names and are working together financially.

This is one of the rare stories where people later realise where they went wrong and actually rectify the problem and get back together. In most cases that would be the end of the family unit.

# TIPS ON DEALING WITH FINANCES IN MARRIAGE

- Feel the sense of belonging: Many marriages that struggle financially are caused by insecurities that deter couples from feeling that they fully belong. If one gets into a marriage expecting to divorce or separate then it becomes difficult to commit your finances where you are not sure of your future. When you feel the sense of belonging it automatically mends the love and unity between a couple. It is therefore very important feel the sense of belonging to each other when you are married.

- Never pull the blanket to one side. Do not be selfish. Sometimes everyone else may seem to be doing alright financially and you think your family is the only family that needs financial attention. I have heard many spouses who send money to their extended families and not to the other's spouse's family. Even if you are the only one working, be fair to yours and your spouse's family. Life has a tendency of changing, you may lose your job and tomorrow you might need your spouse to assist your family in times of financial need.

- Never compare salaries. Money is money, it does not change whether it comes from the president or a bin man. It does not matter how much more you earn than your spouse. Learn to appreciate whatever it is that your spouse brings to the table. At the end it is what you do with the money that matters not where you get it or how much you earn.

- Work together. Couples should share the joy of achieving together. When you work together towards a certain goal, it makes both of you happy and that happiness within further strengthens the bond and the need for each other. Married couples who work together often achieve more and faster in life unlike couples who do not work together.

I will give a simple example of a heavy bag with two handles. If one person carries that bag, it takes him/her more time to reach wherever they want but if two people hold both handles of the bag, it becomes lighter and they are most likely to arrive early. I know it may be challenging to work together sometimes due to different likes and interests but remember every little thing you do as a team always succeeds.

- Be transparent. Transparency is key in a marriage, when couples struggle with transparency, it often presents a lot of unwarranted problems which may take longer to resolve or never at all. When there is transparency in a marriage, there is no room for doubt, it's all in the open. There is nothing as annoying as realising that the person you share your life and love with is not being honest and trustworthy. Even if there is no malice in it, the other spouse may end up thinking there is more that they are not aware of and it is that feeling which creates problems in the home. Being transparent with money contributes to a happy marriage

- Prioritise. Set your priorities right. It is always important to have security in life and when people get married they start to build a life together. When you invest your savings into assets like properties through buying land and building step by step together, a mortgage or purchase a complete house. Putting priorities as a family and working together towards seeing your hard work getting into fruition create a great sense of belonging and the need to do more together. It is quite an enjoyable experience when people plan and see results.

There is nothing wrong buying the latest rides and wearing expensive clothes, however it is also very important to ensure there are plans to establish properties. One thing I learnt is, houses appreciate in value whereas possessions like cars depreciate in value. A family that has a one bedroom flat which fully belongs to them are richer than a family that drives the most expensive cars while living in rented property.

# Five Ways of Managing your Finances

## Collective Approach

The collective approach of managing finances in a marriage is one where both spouses put all their earnings in one basket and budget together. This approach works even when the other spouse is not working. Studies have shown that this approach of managing finances in a marriage is the most effective and even improves the quality of relationship that the couple has.

Some people may say that the collective approach is somewhat boring for those people who feel the need for financial independence where they can just spend money when and how they want. The main advantage of this approach is, it does not only make money matters easier but increases the bond in the family.

Before I got married, I was so independent financially. I would help my parents back home, take trips with friends whenever I wanted, even bought properties without consulting anyone or seeking approval. I enjoyed watching myself save money towards something and I would feel good when I achieved it.

When I got married, I still felt the need to continue with the independence whereby I would do whatever I wanted with the money that I earned. However my dear husband had a different perspective with regard to dealing with finances in a marriage whatsoever. At the onset he told me how important he felt it is that a married couple put their finances together and develop from there. Of course it was difficult for me to just change overnight. After trying it for sometime, I realised it made our goals easier and faster to achieve and it also enabled transparency.

It does not however mean that when you put all your monies in one basket, you cannot have that little extra to pamper yourself or go out for a drink or lunch with friends. Usually within the budget, couples have a certain monthly or weekly or yearly allowance which they can use any way they want without necessarily accounting for it to their spouse.

## Contribute a fixed Amount

Another approach that couples use when they are both working is that they contribute and commit to a fixed amount monthly towards the household upkeep. The remainder each one can do what they desire with it.

This approach can work for some but can also present a big challenge for others. It is important to be disciplined when you use this approach because sometimes the other spouse may struggle with curiosity of wanting to know where and how the other money was spend. This is where you can see challenges of distrust and misery.

If this is however the best way you can manage your finances without any hitches, then God will surely bless your household.

## **Allocate Responsibility**

Allocating responsibility to each other is another approach which couples use. This approach is also for spouses that are both bringing an income. So for example one can cater for rentals/ mortgage and car insurance and the other can cater for kids school fees and food. This can work well if no curiosity of knowing where the other money from your spouse goes. If each of the spouses commit fully to their allocated responsibilities then that should be alright. The most important thing when managing finances is that there should be harmony at the end of it.

## **Use yours I keep mine**

This is the selfish approach in which a spouse feels that they do not have an obligation to contribute their money to the family upkeep and development because it should be done by the other.

This has no doubt the biggest potential of creating marital friction and misery. I have seen couples who withhold finances from their family because they expect the other spouse to do everything. When we look at it, it equates to financial abuse and in most cases it is the children who suffer in the end. This approach I personally do not recommend as it can break the harmony and happiness in the home.

## One Income

When there is one income, my recommendation would be to budget together and work together in achieving your family goals. Traditionally, many families survived on one income. The fathers were the bread winners and the mothers would stay at home taking care of the children and the day to day activities at home. Today has totally changed, wives have also become more and more influential financially such that you find wives as breadwinners in many homes. It however does not matter who is bringing in the cheque, it matters how you plan your finances as a family unit.

## What to do when Your spouse has other children outside your marriage

Many people are getting married with children from previous marriages or relationships. Giving financial support to the children from other relationships has often presented a lot of financial disputes in marriages. Sometimes these disputes end up affecting children more. I have seen children who have well to do fathers and mothers failing to pay school fees or buy school uniforms. It is a sad situation whereby a parent only focuses on the children who she/he lives with. In reality whether you live with your children or not, they are still your children and they deserve to get financial support to sustain them.

## NOTE:

1. Before you get married and start another family again. Make it a priority to discuss how you can maintain financial support to your children. Discuss and agree on the amount that is adequate for the children and put it in writing.

2. Support each other in giving the support to his/her children. As much as it may be difficult to deal with your spouse's ex in executing the support. Show that you care by suggesting a separate savings account for the children's incidentals.

3. Approach the children and talk to them about their needs and what you can manage to contribute with your spouse.

4. Never withhold funds to support the children as a punishment or to deal with your misunderstanding with your spouse.

5. In the event that your funds are for some reason strained, communicate to the children's guardian and prioritise important things like school fees and food.

6. Draft a will outlining their allocated inheritance in the case of death. They are part of your estate, therefore they are equally entitled to anything that you own. A will reduces the likelihood of your children not accessing any thing and it also helps to minimise court disputes.

By showing love and support to your spouse's children, you are investing trust and confidence in your spouse. He or she will have a very high regard of you and can entrust you with anything.

## Chapter 17

# WHEN CHRONIC ILLNESS HITS YOUR MARRIAGE-HOW TO EMBRACE AND DEAL WITH IT

### <u>Dealing with Chronic Illness in the marriage</u>

When couples wed, one of the vows that are most important but which couples do not give much thought about on the alter is, '**In sickness and in health**'. This clause is often brushed off because when we feel healthy today, it never occurs to us that one day a chronic illness can knock at our door and in most cases this happens without much emotional preparation.

Many marriages today have been one way or the other affected by chronic illness of spouse. The main common chronic illnesses include cancer, HIV/AIDS, heart disease, dementia, stroke, diabetes and more.

These conditions vary in the impact they cause in a marriage, I interviewed a couple from Southern Africa who related to me how they overcame HIV in their marriage.

## Real Life Story (pseudo names used)

Sheeba and Paul had met for a short time and felt they belonged together, six months after courtship they got married and lived together happily as any other normal couple. They had children, by the time I went to interview them, their children had come to leave their children at grandma and grandpa's. This couple has already grown old together but in their late 60's they seemed happy and in love with each other.

During pregnancy of their third and last child, Sheeba and Paul were given the news that Sheeba was HIV positive and had to consent to the PMTCT programme to prevent the baby from contracting the virus. This came as a shock to them and by that time, HIV was highly stigmatised in the society and you could not share that with anyone. The society always blamed HIV on promiscuity, so they had to deal with this on their own.

Sheeba advised Paul to get tested too and he was diagnosed HIV positive as well. The world came crumbling down for the family and coping was proving very difficult. Sheeba had a miscarriage due to stress. She got very sick after the miscarriage and had a stroke on her left side. That meant she could not walk or do anything on her own, she needed help from other people to survive.

Paul tried as much as he could to assist the wife but as time went on, he also became too stressed by the whole situation and became very sick as well. Although he could still walk and do a few things on his own, his energy levels were getting lower and lower. The extended family had shunned them because of this illness. 'At some point I wished God could just kill us instantly', said Sarah.

Under that much desperation for help and support, Sheeba got temporary admission to the hospital and during one of the visiting hours, a neighbouring church group came to her ward to pray for the patients and among the group was a community worker who was working for an organisation that offered support to HIV/AIDS patients. She promised to come and visit Sheeba again on a different date on her own. She introduced them to the then new drug Antiretroviral which could help boost people's immune system. As much as Sheeba and Paul had almost given up on life, they were ready to try anything.

Although Sheeba continued to be partially paralysed, her health had taken a huge turn to recovery. Paul was also responding very well to the medication. They were introduced to a community support group where they would share their stories and encourage each other.

Paul would help Sheeba to walk and the children did most of the chores in the house. They did not have much money to afford house help but they managed on their own. Paul and Sheeba agreed that they always enjoy talking about their life and laugh at funny occurrences in their life. One of the things they enjoy everyday is when they sit and eat together, sometimes Paul feeds Sheeba not because she cannot feed herself but for the love and care he has for her.

They have lived for a little over thirty years with HIV and they live a happy life and pray together everyday.

This story is not just an encouragement to couples that are experiencing chronic illness in their marriage. It is also meant to prepare young people contemplating marriage on the challenges that can befall any couple. It also serves to highlight the importance of getting tested early for chronic illnesses. That way you can stand a chance getting better medical care before the conditions get to a dire state.

Further, my advice especially to the young people preparing to get married is, get tested before you get married. I have met several young couples who ended up divorcing because they discovered they had HIV after marriage. It normally provokes the blame game whereby one suspects the other for adultery or sleeping around before marriage.

Overall, having HIV or any other chronic illness does not necessarily mean the end of the world. Do not lose hope because you have tested positive for a chronic illness. There are many people who are surviving and living happier lives today.

## How to Deal with Chronic Illness in your marriage:

## Acceptance

The first step in any kind of challenge with illness or other devastating situations that we face in life is the capability to accept the situation. Acceptance enables a person to digest and deal with the phase of denial after being diagnosed with any chronic illness. It means allowing yourself to be bigger than the situation. This serves to both parties, the infected party and the affected party. In most cases it is the affected party that tends to suffer more when their spouse is diagnosed with a chronic illness. Many questions begin to surface in mind, how do I deal with this, how do we cope, is he/she going to die soon, are we going to continue to be intimate?

After the phase of questioning yourself comes the reality of actually dealing with it.

## Support System

Any couple, nomatter how strong and well organised you may be, you need a good and strong support system and by that I do not mean just the family or friends. You need family or friends who are willing to be there for you through thick and thin. There is no need for a thousand visits or a thousand friends to surround you, you can have one or two friends or families who can fulfil the support you require. It is important to have people who truly understand your situation. They may not offer much in terms of making you feel better but they can surely help you cope and live life happily.

Nowadays most clinics and hospitals that deal with chronic illness have centres which offer support groups for people experiencing the same illness. Within these support groups, there are many activities that members get involved in which enable people to cope and to encourage each other on best ways to deal with their illness. In most cases, married couples attend these support groups together.

## Assurance

There is a high percentage of couples who have gone their separate ways because of insecurities. I have heard cases where a spouse feels inadequate to their spouse because they are ill and as a result they started to behave irrationally to the spouse giving them support.

In the end the pressure becomes too much for the spouse to bear and have ended in separation or divorce or even early death caused by grief and stress.

Constantly giving assurance to your spouse that you care and love them nomatter what and this should be stamped by action that you show. One thing is saying I care and then the next minute you leave your spouse without the required care. Action in this case must prevail more as a form of assuring your spouse that you are there to stay.

## Continue to be Intimate

I have highlighted the different types of intimacy in a marriage in chapter 15. Intimacy plays a very big role in a marriage and it is one of the highest causes of insecurities when one has an illness that limits them in doing what they would normally do without the illness. However being ill does not mean the end of an intimate life, it only means things may be done differently. Taking time to just sit and cuddle each other, kiss, hold hands, go for a walk are all forms of intimacy that can strengthen the bond between a married couple.

## Stay positive

According to Focus on Family article 2008, it says refuse to be owned by your condition. Life, nomatter how painful or confusing, is precious and worth living. Do your best to make lemonade out of lemons and rest at His feet when you are wrung-out.

My husband always says in our normal day to day life, let us celebrate each day that we are together, because tomorrow is not guaranteed to anyone. This statement has been our reference point even in times where we are faced with challenges, we always try to look at the brighter side of life.

## Pray

God's line is always open, prayer is healing, it is intimate, it is unity and love. My best friend always says, you never go wrong with prayer. Praying together for healing and comfort can surely change your life positively. The more you spend time in prayer, the less you dwell on the illness. If you have a church support group, it is also a good platform to share prayers and things to pray for. Remember prayer is everything, it shadows all our grievances and restores where we are broken.

Printed in the United States
By Bookmasters